THE LITTLE BOOK OF

OF

MARKET MYTHS

Little Book Big Profits Series

In the *Little Book Big Profits* series, the brightest icons in the financial world write on topics that range from tried-and-true investment strategies to tomorrow's new trends. Each book offers a unique perspective on investing, allowing the reader to pick and choose from the very best in investment advice today.

Books in the *Little Book Big Profits* series include:

The Little Book That Still Beats the Market by Joel Greenblatt
The Little Book of Value Investing by Christopher Browne
The Little Book of Common Sense Investing by John C. Bogle
The Little Book That Makes You Rich by Louis Navellier
The Little Book That Builds Wealth by Pat Dorsey
The Little Book That Saves Your Assets by David M. Darst
The Little Book of Bull Moves by Peter D. Schiff
The Little Book of Main Street Money by Jonathan Clements
The Little Book of Safe Money by Jason Zweig
The Little Book of Behavioral Investing by James Montier
The Little Book of Big Dividends by Charles B. Carlson
The Little Book of Bulletproof Investing by Ben Stein and Phil DeMuth
The Little Book of Commodity Investing by John R. Stephenson
The Little Book of Economics by Greg Ip
The Little Book of Sideways Markets by Vitaliy N. Katsenelson
The Little Book of Currency Trading by Kathy Lien
The Little Book of Stock Market Profits by Mitch Zacks
The Little Book of Big Profits from Small Stocks by Hilary Kramer
The Little Book of Trading by Michael W. Covel
The Little Book of Alternative Investments by Ben Stein and Phil DeMuth
The Little Book of Valuation by Aswath Damodaran
The Little Book of Emerging Markets by Mark Mobius
The Little Book of Hedge Funds by Anthony Scaramucci
The Little Book of the Shrinking Dollar by Addison Wiggin
The Little Book of Bull's Eye Investing by John Mauldin
The Little Book of Market Myths by Ken Fisher and Lara Hoffmans

THE LITTLE BOOK

OF

MARKET MYTHS

*How to Profit by Avoiding
the Investing Mistakes
Everyone Else Makes*

KEN FISHER
LARA HOFFMANS

WILEY

John Wiley & Sons, Inc.

Contents

Preface   ix

Chapter One
Bonds Are Safer Than Stocks   1

Chapter Two
Asset Allocation Short-Cuts   17

Chapter Three
Volatility and Only Volatility   27

Chapter Four
More Volatile Than Ever   37

Chapter Five
**The Holy Grail—Capital Preservation
and Growth**   49

Chapter Six
The GDP–Stock Mismatch Crash   55

Chapter Seven
10% Forever!   67

Chapter Eight
High Dividends for Sure Income   75

Chapter Nine
The Perma-Superiority of Small-Cap Value   83

Chapter Ten
Wait Until You're Sure   93

Chapter Eleven
Stop-Losses Stop Losses   105

Chapter Twelve
High Unemployment Kills Stocks   113

Chapter Thirteen
Over-Indebted America   131

Chapter Fourteen
Strong Dollar, Strong Stocks   153

Chapter Fifteen
Turmoil Troubles Stocks   161

Chapter Sixteen
News You Can Use   171

Chapter Seventeen
Too Good to Be True   181

Notes   191

Acknowledgments   201

About the Authors   205

Preface

QUESTIONING YOURSELF IS HARD.

One of the hardest things we do (or rather, don't do). Folks don't like questioning themselves. If we question, we might discover we're wrong, causing humiliation and pain. Humans evolved over many millennia to take any number of extraordinary and often irrational steps to avoid even the risk of humiliation and pain.

Those instincts likely helped our long-distant ancestors avoid being mauled by wild beasts and starving through long winters. But these deeply imprinted instincts often are exactly wrong when it comes to more modern problems like frequently counterintuitive capital markets.

I often say investing success is two-thirds avoiding mistakes, one-third doing something right. If you can just avoid mistakes, you can lower your error rate. That alone should improve your results. If you can avoid mistakes *and* do something right on occasion, you likely do better than most everyone. Better than most professionals!

Maybe you think avoiding mistakes is easy. Just don't make mistakes! Who sets out to make them, anyway? But investors don't make mistakes because they know they're mistakes. They make them because they think they're making smart decisions. Decisions they've made plenty of times and have seen other smart people make. They think they're the right decisions because they don't question.

After all, what sense does it make to question something that "everyone knows"? Or something that's common sense? Or something you learned from someone supposedly smarter than you?

Waste of time, right?

No! You should always question *everything* you think you know. Not once, but every time you make an investing decision. It's not hard. Well, functionally it's not hard, though emotionally and instinctually, it might be. What's the worst that can happen? You discover you were right all along, which is fun. No harm done. No humiliation!

Or ... you discover you were wrong. And not just you, but the vast swaths of humanity who believe a false truth—just as you did! You've uncovered a mythology. And discovering something you previously thought to be true is actually myth saves you from making a potentially costly mistake (or making it again). That's not humiliating, that's beautiful. And potentially profitable.

The good news is, once you start questioning, it gets easier. You may think it impossible to do. After all, if it were easy, wouldn't everyone do it? (Answer: No. Most people prefer the easy route of never questioning and never being humiliated.) But you can question anything and everything—and should. Start with those things you read in the paper or hear on TV and nod along with. If you're nodding, you've found a truth you've probably never investigated much, if at all.

Like the near-universal belief high unemployment is economically bad and a stock market killer. I know of no one who says the reverse—that high unemployment doesn't cause future economic doom. Yet, as I show in Chapter 12, unemployment is provably a late, lagging indicator and not indicative of future economic or market direction. And amazingly, recessions start when unemployment is at or near cyclical lows, not the reverse. The data prove that, and fundamentally it makes sense, once you start thinking how a CEO would (as I explain in the book). This is a myth I disprove using pretty easy-to-get data from public sources. Data that's universally available and easy to compile! But few question this myth, so it endures.

This book covers some of the most widely believed market and economic myths—ones that routinely cause folks to see the world wrongly, leading to investing errors. Like America has "too much" debt, age should dictate asset allocation, high dividend stocks can produce reliable retirement income, stop-losses actually stop losses and more. Many I've written about before in various books, but here I collect what I view as the most egregious myths and expand on them or use a different angle or updated data.

Then, too, I've written about many of these myths before simply because they *are* so widely and rigidly and wrongly believed. My guess is writing about them here again won't convince many (or even most) the mythology is wrong. They'll prefer the easy route and the mythology. And that's ok. Because you may prefer the truth—which gives you an edge—a way to avoid making investment decisions based not on sound analysis and/or fundamental theory, but on a myth everyone believes just because.

Each chapter in the book is dedicated to one myth. Jump around! Read them all or just those that interest you. Either way, I hope the book helps you improve your investing results by helping you see the world a bit clearer. And I hope the examples included here inspire you to do some sleuthing on your own so you can uncover still more market mythology.

You'll quickly see a few common characteristics throughout the chapters. A how-to manual to myth debunking, if you will. The tactics I use over and over to debunk these myths include:

Just asking *if something is true*. The first, most basic step. If you can't do this, you can't move to later steps.

Being counterintuitive. If "everyone knows" something, ask if the reverse might be true.

Checking history. Maybe everyone says XYZ just happened, and that's bad. Or it would be so much better if ABC happened. Maybe that's true, maybe not. You can check history to see if XYZ reliably led to bad or ABC to good. Ample free historical data exist for you to do this!

Running some simple correlations. If everyone believes X causes Y, you can check if it always does, sometimes does or never does.

Scaling. If some number seems impossibly scary and large, put it in proper context. It may bring that fear down to size.

Thinking globally. Folks often presume the US is an island. It's not—the US is heavily impacted by what happens outside its borders. And investors the world over tend to have similar fears, motivations, etc.

There are plenty of myths investors fall prey to—I couldn't possibly cover them all here. But if you can get in your bones the beauty and power of questioning, over time, you should be fooled less by harmful myth and get better long-term results. So here we go.

Chapter One

Bonds Are Safer Than Stocks

"Everyone knows bonds are safer than stocks."

You've heard that said so often, maybe it doesn't seem worth investigating. With 2008 still fresh in most investors' minds, it may seem sacrilegious to even question this. (Another odd behavioral quirk: Stocks were up huge in 2009 and 2010, flattish in 2011, and up again in 2012 as I write. Yet the bad returns five years back loom so much larger in our brains than the four subsequent years of overall big positive returns.)

But those beliefs that are so widely, broadly, universally held are often those that end up being utterly wrong—even backward.

Go ahead. Ask, "Are they?"

And initially, it may seem intuitive that plodding bonds are safer than stocks with their inherent wild wiggles. But I say, whether bonds are safer or not can depend on what you mean by "safe."

There's no technical definition—there's huge room for interpretation. For example, one person might think "safe" means a low level of expected shorter-term volatility. No wiggles! Another person might think "safe" means an increased likelihood he achieves long-term goals, which may require a higher level of shorter-term volatility.

Bonds Are Volatile, Too

People often make the error of thinking bonds aren't volatile. Not so. Bonds have price volatility, too. And their prices move in inverse relationship to interest rates. When interest rates rise, prices of currently issued bonds fall, and vice versa. So from year to year, as interest rates for varying categories of bonds move up and down, their prices move down and up. Some categories of bonds are more volatile than others—but in any given year, bonds can have negative returns—even US Treasurys.

But overall, as a broader category, bonds typically aren't as volatile as stocks—*over shorter time periods.*

That's an important caveat. *Over shorter time periods* like a year or even five, bonds are less volatile. They have lower expected returns, too. But if your exclusive goal is avoiding much volatility, and you don't care about superior long-term returns, that may not bother you.

Exhibit 1.1 shows average annual returns and standard deviation (a common measure of volatility) over five-year rolling periods. It's broken into a variety of

Exhibit 1.1   Five-Year Time Horizon—Volatility

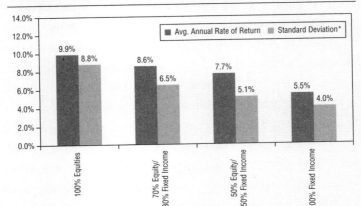

*Standard deviation represents the degree of fluctuations in historical returns. This risk measure is applied to five-year annualized rolling returns in the chart.

Source: Global Financial Data, Inc., as of 06/22/2012. US 10-Year Government Bond Index, S&P 500 Total Return Index, average rate of return for rolling 5-year periods from 12/31/25 through 12/31/11.[1]

allocations, including 100% stocks, 70% stocks/30% fixed income, 50%/50% and 100% fixed income.

Returns were superior for 100% stocks. And, not surprising, average standard deviation was higher for 100% stocks than for any allocation with fixed income—meaning stocks were more volatile on average. The more fixed income in the allocation over rolling five-year periods, the lower the average standard deviation.

So far, I haven't said anything that surprises you. *Everyone knows* stocks are more volatile than bonds.

Stocks Are Less Volatile Than Bonds?

But hang on—if you increase your observation period, something happens. Exhibit 1.2 shows the same thing as Exhibit 1.1, but over rolling 20-year periods. Standard deviation for 100% stocks fell materially and was near identical to standard deviation for 100% fixed income. Returns were still superior for stocks—*but with similar historic volatility.*

It gets more pronounced over 30-year time periods—shown in Exhibit 1.3. (If you think 30 years is an impossibly long investing time horizon, see Chapter 2. Investors commonly assume a too-short time horizon—a 30-year time horizon likely isn't unreasonable for most readers of this book.) Over rolling 30-year periods historically, average standard deviation for

Exhibit 1.2   20-Year Time Horizon—Volatility

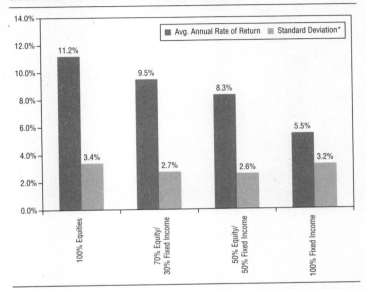

*Standard deviation represents the degree of fluctuations in historical returns. This risk measure is applied to 20-year annualized rolling returns in the chart.
Source: Global Financial Data, Inc.; as of 06/22/2012. US 10-Year Government Bond Index, S&P 500 Total Return Index, average rate of return for rolling 20-year periods from 12/31/25 through 12/31/11.[2]

100% stocks was *lower* than for 100% fixed income. Stocks had *half* the volatility but much better returns!

Day to day, month to month and year to year, stocks can experience tremendous volatility—often much more than bonds. It can be emotionally tough to experience—but that higher shorter-term volatility shouldn't surprise you. Finance theory says it should be

Exhibit 1.3   30-Year Time Horizon—Volatility

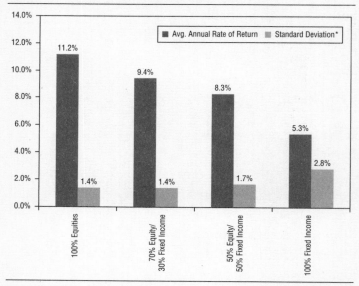

*Standard deviation represents the degree of fluctuations in historical returns. This risk measure is applied to 30-year annualized rolling returns in the chart.

Source: Global Financial Data, Inc.; as of 06/22/2012. US 10-Year Government Bond Index, S&P 500 Total Return Index, average rate of return for rolling 30-year periods from 12/31/25 through 12/31/11.[3]

so. To get to stocks' long-term superior returns over fixed income, you must accept a higher degree of shorter-term volatility. If stocks were less volatile year to year on average, their returns would likely be lower. Like bonds!

But given a bit more time, those monthly and yearly wild wiggles resolve into steadier and more consistent *upward* volatility. And yes, volatility goes both ways. You probably don't hear this often (if ever), but *data prove stocks have been less volatile than bonds* historically over longer periods—*and* with superior returns.

Blame Evolution

If that's the case, why do so many investors fear stocks? Easy: evolution.

It's been proven that investors feel the pain of loss over twice as intensely as they enjoy the pleasure of gain. That's from the Nobel Prize–winning behavioral finance concept of *prospect theory*. Another way to say that is it's natural for danger (or perceived danger) to loom larger in our brains than the prospect of safety.

This evolved response no doubt treated our long-distant ancestors well. Folks who naturally fretted, constantly, the threat of attack by saber-toothed tigers were likely better off than their more lackadaisical peers. (The best way to win a fight with a saber-toothed tiger is not to get into one.) And those who had an outsized fear of the coming winter likely prepared better and faced lower freezing and/or starving risk. Hence, they more successfully passed on their more vigilant genes. But obsessing about future pleasantness or the absence of freezing risk didn't really help perpetuate the species.

And our basic brain functioning just hasn't changed that much in the evolutionary blink-of-an-eye since. Which is why it's been proven a 10% portfolio loss feels about as bad to US investors on average as a 25% gain feels good. (European investors feel the pain of loss even more intensely.)

Stocks Are Positive Much More Often Than Not

What has that to do with the common misperception stocks are just down a lot? Exhibit 1.4 shows how often stocks are positive versus negative over varying time periods. On a daily basis, the odds stocks are positive are slightly better than a coin flip. And negative days tend to come in clumps. Positive days, too! But because we're hyper-aware of danger, the negative clumps loom bigger in our brains, even though that's not what reality is.

Behaviorally, it can be very difficult not to think so short term. But if you can stretch your observation period just a bit longer, odds are good stocks will be positive. Stocks are positive historically in 62% of calendar months—though they come in clumps, too. Rolling 12-month periods are positive 73.2% of the

Exhibit 1.4   Stocks' Historical Frequency of Positive Returns

	Number of Periods			Percent of Periods	
	Positive	Negative	Total	Positive	Negative
Daily Returns*	11,526	10,224	21,750	53.0%	47.0%
Calendar Month Returns	640	391	1,031	62.1%	37.9%
Calendar Quarter Returns	233	110	343	67.9%	32.1%
Calendar Year Returns	61	24	85	71.8%	28.2%
Rolling 1-Year Returns	747	273	1,020	73.2%	26.8%
Rolling 5-Year Returns**	843	129	972	86.7%	13.3%
Rolling 10-Year Returns**	858	54	912	94.1%	5.9%
Rolling 20-Year Returns**	792	0	792	100.0%	0.0%
Rolling 25-Year Returns**	732	0	732	100.0%	0.0%

*Daily return data begin 1/1/1928 and are based on price appreciation only; all other data begin 1/31/1926 and reflect total return.

**Measured monthly.

Source: Global Financial Data, Inc., as of 6/27/2012. S&P 500 Total Return Index from 01/31/1926 to 12/31/2011.[4]

time. And yet, media headlines and pundits hyperventilate as if there's a bear lurking around every corner. What they should really fear is missing market upside (see Chapter 3), but that isn't what comes naturally to our brains—which aren't all that different from our distant ancestors' caveman brains.

History is clear—stocks are positive much more than not on average. And over longer periods like 20 years or more, they're actually *less* volatile than bonds. It can be difficult to overcome ingrained behavior and think that way, but if you can, the long-term rewards are likely to be better with stocks (if you have a well-diversified portfolio, of course) than with bonds.

Stocks Are Positive—And Overwhelmingly Beat Bonds

But some folks just have a hard time battling millennia of cognitive evolution and can't stop thinking, "What if?" What if stocks buck the odds and do terribly ahead? Let's look at just what the odds are.

Investing is about probabilities, not certainties. There are no certainties in investing—not even in Treasurys, which can lose value in any given year. You must rationally assess probabilities of outcomes based on history, basic economic fundamentals and what you know about current conditions.

Odds are, if you have a long time horizon, stocks are likelier to outperform bonds. But what if they don't? There have been 67 rolling 20-year periods since 1926 (as far back as we have very good US data, which can serve as a reasonable proxy for world stocks). Stocks beat bonds in 65 of them (97%). Over 20 years, stocks returned an average 881% and bonds 247%—stocks beat bonds by a 3.6-to-1 margin.[5] Pretty darn good! When bonds beat stocks, however, it was by just a

1.1-to-1 margin on average—and stocks were still positive, averaging 243% to bonds' 262%.[6]

In Vegas, the lower the probability, the bigger the potential payout. Yet this is the opposite of how the stock-versus-bond decision typically works. (Another reason why folks who compare investing to gambling are hugely wide of the mark.) Incidentally, over 30-year rolling periods, bonds have never beat stocks. Stocks returned an average 2,428% to bonds' 550%—a 4.5-to-1 outperformance margin.[7]

So, yes, over shorter time periods, bonds on average have materially lower volatility characteristics. Some people might call that "safe." But if your goal is to generate higher returns over long periods to increase the likelihood of achieving your goals, the shorter-term lower volatility of bonds may be less appropriate. And 20 or 30 years later, if you discover your portfolio hasn't grown enough to meet your goals, you may not feel so safe—particularly since over that longer time period, stocks are likely to be less volatile on average.

The Stock Evolution

Data and history prove stocks have had superior long-term returns. But there's an additional reason to believe stocks are likely to have superior returns over long periods moving forward: Stocks evolve.

Stocks are a piece of ownership in a firm. Taken together, stocks represent the collective wisdom of the business world. And they represent the promise of future technological advances and future profits from those innovations.

Businesses and, hence, stocks adapt. Some businesses don't survive. They fail—but get replaced by something newer, better, more efficient. That's creative destruction, and it's a powerful force for societal good.

And firms will always be motivated to chase future profits. Whatever problems get in our way—energy, food, water, disease—someone (or someones) will find ways to collide past innovations in new ways to yield something new that can knock down or at least greatly mitigate whatever problems pop up. How can you know this? Because it's always been that way.

In 1798, the Reverend Thomas Malthus predicted food production would soon peak—there was simply no way in his (rather unimaginative) mind the world could produce enough to feed much more than a billion people. He outright rejected the notion of "unlimited progress" in food production.

Yet, six billion more people later, and in much of the developed world, the greater problem we face is obesity. Yes, in some emerging nations, famine is still a problem. But that's nearly entirely a factor of poor governance. The world has more than enough food—we need more freedom and democracy so poor, oppressed nations needn't rely on corrupt governments and their failing infrastructure to distribute food to the populace.

Time and again, folks with dire, long-term forecasts are proven wrong because they rely on poor assumptions that ignore future innovations and the power of profit motive. My favorite was the fellow who, in 1894, predicted London's growing population and industry would require so much horse power, by 1950, London would be covered in nine feet of manure![8]

How on earth could he have predicted the combustion-engine revolution that would soon render horse-drawn transportation a quaint relic? He couldn't have, but he might have had more faith in the transformational power unleashed by folks eager to chase profits.

The wildly popular 1968 book *Population Bomb* assured us that in the 1970s, famine would kill hundreds of millions. Didn't happen, thanks to Norman Borlaug (a guy who truly deserved his Nobel Peace prize) and his dwarf wheat—not to mention agricultural innovators who preceded him over multiple millennia.

Folks who believe ardently Peak Oil (the point at which conventional oil production peaks) will be the death of us miss this, too. Many perfectly rational folks

posit conventional oil production has already peaked—
some pin it sometime in the 1970s, others in the 1980s,
1990s and even more recently. Feel free to quibble with
any of these. And whenever you think it happened, you
can blame it on whatever you want (in the US, for
example, you might blame the creation of the EPA,
which put severe restrictions on production). But even
if you believe we hit peak production in the 1970s,
what terrible thing has happened since? In 1980, global
GDP was about $10.7 trillion; now it's about $71.3
trillion.[9] Life expectancies have extended. Per capita
income has skyrocketed across many emerging markets.
We've done ok. Sure, we've had bear markets and
recessions—some bigger, some smaller. But that's true
of any longer time period.

And known reserves of oil are *double* what they were
in 1980, yet consumption has only, overall and on average, increased over that time. Technological advances
have allowed us not just to discover more oil and natural
gas, but to innovate ways to extract both from spots
once thought unrecoverable.

Many Peak Oilers will argue supply has nothing to
do with production. That's merely a misunderstanding
of basic economics. If the supply exists, and prices make
future (conventional or unconventional) extraction
profitable, producers will extract. Or innovate still more

new ways to extract. Or if extraction truly becomes unprofitable (which I doubt happens for a long time), my hypothesis (based on observation of the entire history of humanity) is we'll innovate ways to get more energy efficient. Or find substitutes. True depletion is such a long way off, we have plenty of time to innovate the next solution (or solutions). If you don't believe that, check London, which isn't buried under nine feet of manure.

That transformational power unleashed by profit motive is encapsulated by stocks. Bonds are fine, but they don't represent future earnings. Bonds are a contract. You buy a bond, you get that yield—that's it. But future earnings eventually improve, as they always have and always will—that's captured in stocks.

Think of Moore's Law—the idea the number of transistors on an integrated circuit should double about every two years—conceived by Gordon Moore, co-founder of Intel in 1965. There's also Kryder's Law, which proved in 2005 hard-drive memory storage is moving at a much faster pace than Moore's Law—and that's likely to continue or even accelerate! And then there's the Shannon-Hartley Theorem, which states the maximum rate information can be transmitted over a communications channel (think fiber optics) is also increasing exponentially.

What does all that mean? We conceive of progress as linear, when it's really exponential—and the collision of all these technologies means future innovation will move faster, as technologies conceived by people unknown to each other in far-flung locations collide in perfectly unpredictable ways to produce the next life-saving or -improving technology or process.

If you think today's electronic gadgets represent the pinnacle of human ingenuity, you'll be proven wrong. I don't know when or how, but I needn't know—I can just own stocks and benefit. Human nature hasn't changed enough that folks won't be self-motivated to use their ingenuity to devise solutions to profit from problems. Always been that way. And those who profit most from innovation aren't the technologists. No, they're those who learn to package, market and sell those innovations—and their shareholders.

Chapter Two

Asset Allocation Short-Cuts

~

"Take 100, subtract your age.
That's what you should
have in stocks. Easy!"

HUMANS LOVE SHORT-CUTS. Even in investing! We want to believe there's an easier way. Just look at the proliferation of "lose-weight-fast" gimmicks. And there are a million "get-rich-quick" schemes (which are mostly scams—more in Chapter 17).

A popular short-cut in financial planning circles is the idea you can *take 100, subtract your age, and that's how much you should have in stocks*. You can read that rule of thumb in magazines, blogs—even some professionals adhere to it!

There are variations—some say "take 120." (Already you should be skeptical of a rule of thumb with an inherent 20% swing in asset allocation depending on which one you follow.)

This bit of investing non-wisdom persists because it seems simple. Concrete! Straightforward. It's a fast and easy solution to the very serious issue of asset allocation. But be wary of anything regarding your long-term financial planning that seems fast and easy. More broadly, investing rules of thumb should be regarded with severe cynicism, if not ignored outright.

The Critical Asset Allocation Decision

Long-term asset allocation decisions are, in fact, important. Most investing professionals today agree the long-term asset allocation decision is the most critical one investors make. Many point to an academic study that found about 90% of a portfolio's return over time can be attributed to asset allocation—the mix of stocks/bonds/cash/other securities and in what percentages.[1]

At my firm, we take this a step further. You can think of it like the funnel in Exhibit 2.1. We believe 70% of portfolio performance is driven by the asset allocation decision—the mix of stocks/bonds/cash/other

Exhibit 2.1   Asset Allocation Impact—70/20/10

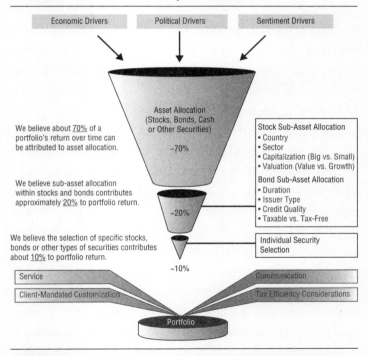

Note: Forward-looking return attribution is an approximation intended for illustrative purposes and should not be considered a forecast of future returns or return attribution.

securities. We believe 20% of portfolio performance is driven by *sub-asset* allocation—the subsequent decisions on *categories* of securities—size, style, country, sector, industry, credit rating, duration, etc. The final 10% of performance over long periods on average is driven by the selection of individual securities, i.e., whether you hold Pepsi or Coke, Merck or Pfizer, an IBM bond or Microsoft, etc.

Either way, few argue the asset-allocation decision isn't key for long-term success. So why would anyone relegate it to a simplistic rule of thumb? Folks who believe this believe age—and age *alone*—is the only factor that matters. One thing!

That cookie-cutter way of thinking presumes everyone of a same age is identical. I can think of few rules of thumb more potentially injurious. This ignores things like investors' goals, how much cash flow they may need now or in the future and how much growth is appropriate for their goals. It ignores current circumstances, portfolio size, whether the investor is still working or not. It ignores myriad more details unique to that investor. And *it ignores the spouse!* I've learned a tremendous amount in my long professional investing career—perhaps one of the more important lessons is *never forget the spouse*. That's a good rule for your personal life, too.

Yes, age matters. It figures into investing time horizon. But time horizon is just one factor that should be considered alongside and in concert with things like return expectations, cash flow needs, current circumstances, etc. (For more, see my 2012 book, *Plan Your Prosperity*.) This rule of thumb by definition ignores all that.

Getting Time Horizon Right

Even if I can get folks to stop thinking about *age* and start thinking about *time horizon*—and if I can get them to accept that time horizon is an important factor but just one and not the sole driving factor for asset allocation—much too often, folks think about time horizon wrong.

Folks often think this way: "I'm 60. I plan to retire at 65, so I have a five-year time horizon." They think of time horizon stretching out to retirement day, or the day they plan to start taking cash flow or some other milestone. To me, this form of thinking potentially cuts you off at the knees and leads to errors. Worse, those errors may not become apparent until years later—often too late to do much about them.

Time horizon isn't the period of time between now and some milestone. Time horizon is *how long you need your assets to work for you*. For many individual investors, this is often their whole life and that of their spouse. *Never forget the spouse.*

Exhibit 2.2 shows average life expectancy, straight from the Social Security Administration's actuaries. If you're a 60-year-old man in the US, Social Security estimates your average life expectancy is another 21 years on average. If you're a 60-year-old woman, your estimated average life expectancy is another 24 years.

Is that *your* time horizon? Maybe. Do you think you're average? If you're in good health, active and have parents still alive in their late 80s, you could easily beat the odds—that could mean a 30-year (or more) time horizon.

Exhibit 2.2   Life Expectancy Keeps Getting Longer

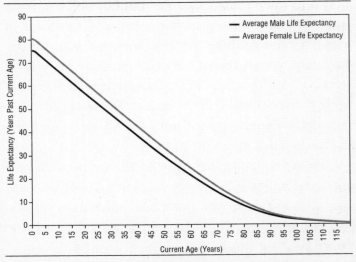

Source: US Social Security Administration, Period Life Table as of 2007.

Unless, for example, you're a 60-year-old man married to a 55-year-old woman—also healthy and active. Her parents, both in their 80s, are still alive. And her grandparents died in their 90s—longevity is in her DNA. That's a potential 40-year time horizon or more—depending on what your other goals are. If your goal is to pass as much as you can to children, you may want to think longer than 40 years. If your goal is to support just the two of you through retirement, think more along the lines of your own life expectancies.

Could both of you die earlier, thwarting your planning? Of course. But dying with ample money in the bank isn't a function of bad planning. What you don't want to do is plan for a 25-year time horizon, get to 85 and discover the money has largely run out. You won't enjoy that. And if your spouse lives to 95, he or she really won't enjoy that—aged poverty is cruel.

Inflation's Insidious Impact

One of the bigger mistakes investors make is underestimating their time horizons and failing to plan for enough growth to accomplish their goals. Many investors assume they don't have big growth goals but fail to remember (1) inflation's insidious impact, and (2) inflation doesn't impact all categories equally.

Over time, inflation can take a serious whack at your purchasing power. Say you need $50,000 today to cover your living expenses. In 10 years, if inflation is anything like its long-term historic average (about 3% annually),[2] you'll need over $67,000. And in 20 years, you'll need $90,142. (See Exhibit 2.3.)

If you're a 60 year old in good health, living another 30 years is certainly possible. If you're 50, living another 30 would be unremarkable. To maintain the purchasing power of your $50,000, in 30 years, you'll need $121,034! If you're relying on your portfolio to kick off all or part of the cash flow needed to cover living expenses and you have a long time horizon, you

Exhibit 2.3   Maintaining Purchasing Power

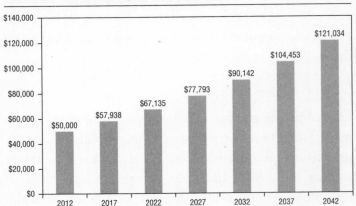

Source: Global Financial Data, Inc., as of 05/22/2012; CPI annualized rate of return from 12/31/1925 to 12/31/2011 was 3.0%.

likely need some growth, just to increase the odds your portfolio stretches enough so your cash flow keeps pace with inflation. By underestimating your time horizon and underestimating how much growth you need, you could increase the odds your portfolio is unable to kick off the level of cash flow you had been counting on. And if you discover that 10 or 20 years down the road, you may not be able to do much about it.

Then, too, you want to assume a life expectancy a bit on the long side and, therefore, your time horizon (if your time horizon is driven by your life expectancy and/or that of your spouse).

Why? Life expectancy keeps expanding! In every decade, average life expectancy has increased. New technologies and medical discoveries have made longer life not just possible, but more pleasant. Not only do we have better cures and maintenance medicines for many diseases once considered an immediate death sentence— we have better ways to detect cancer, heart disease, etc., earlier. And don't dismiss the importance of mobility. Folks who are mobile live longer—and great strides in joint replacement and prosthetics have allowed folks to maintain greater mobility much longer. A body that moves has a healthier heart.

And that innovation likely won't stop in the period ahead (for reasons covered in Chapter 1). Which means it's very likely life expectancies keep expanding, and your time horizon should allow for that.

And, as said earlier, time horizon is just one key consideration in determining an appropriate long-term asset allocation (i.e., benchmark). It's an important factor, but not the sole factor and must be considered alongside return expectations, cash flow needs, current circumstances and any other unique personal factors. Which makes determining asset allocation by age and age alone a rule of thumb you can give the boot.

Chapter Three

Volatility and Only Volatility

~

"Volatility is the most important risk investors face."

QUICK! WHEN I SAY, "Investment risk," what comes to mind? Naturally and instinctively, for most readers, it's, "Volatility!"

Many investors act as though "risk" and "volatility" are interchangeable. And they often are! Volatility is a key risk that investors should consider (though, often, it can matter over what time period you consider volatility, as discussed in Chapter 1). And volatility is the risk that, most of the time and over shorter periods, investors feel most keenly.

It can be heart-stopping to watch your equity allocation—whether it's 100% of your portfolio or just 10%—lose up to 20% fast, as can happen in corrections. And even more grinding to watch it fall 30%, 40% or more in a big bear market. Ultimately, equity investors put up with volatility because finance theory says (and history has supported), long term, you should get rewarded for that volatility—more so than in other, less volatile asset classes.

But volatility isn't the only risk investors face. There are myriad! As discussed in Chapter 1, folks often believe bonds are *safer*. But there's no universally accepted, technical definition of *safe*. And no bond is risk free. Bond investors face *default risk*—the risk the debt issuer delays payments or even goes bankrupt! It happens—even to highly rated firms. Default risk in US Treasurys is exceptionally low—so much so professionals often refer to it as the "risk-free" rate.

Oft-Overlooked Interest Rate Risk

But that's not exactly right. Why? There's also *interest rate risk*—the risk interest rates' moving in either direction impacts your return. In falling interest rate environments, investors may find it difficult to roll over funds from maturing bonds into something with a similar yield. If you bought a 10-year bond with a 5% coupon in 2003, your only option as it matures in 2013 is likely to accept a much lower coupon rate. Or if you want the 5% coupon, your option is likely a bond with a riskier profile or a longer term, which can also ratchet risk. Either way, it's not an apples-to-apples rollover.

That's one half of interest rate risk. As I write in 2012, interest rates across the board are lower than they've been as long as most readers have been adults. Maybe lower than they've been in your lifetime! Exhibit 3.1 shows yields on 10-year Treasurys since 1980—rates have fallen with volatility nearly the entire time to generational lows.

That rates are low doesn't mean they must rise soon. They could bump along sideways. Heck, they could go a bit lower still. But, with 10-year Treasurys yielding under 2%, there's not room for them to fall much.

Still, at some future point, interest rates will rise again. I can't say when or how fast. I rather doubt we see the sky-high interest rates we saw in the 1970s and early 1980s again—at least not very soon. Über-high rates then were the function mostly of disastrous monetary policy in the 1970s. Monetary policy in the US and most developed nations has overall improved since as we have more data and better communication

Exhibit 3.1   10-Year Treasury Yields Since 1980

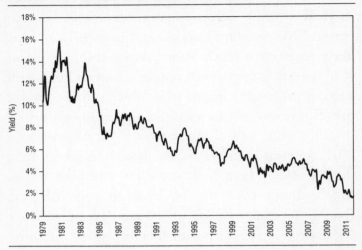

Source: Global Financial Data, Inc., as of 10/25/12, USA 10-Year Bond Constant Maturity Yield from 12/01/79 to 09/30/12.

and coordination. Though Ben Bernanke has made some pretty dumb moves. But even "Helicopter Ben" hasn't been as bad as some of the past outright disaster Fed heads (ahem, Arthur Burns), though Ben still has time, and history will tell.

If the market believes inflation will rise materially in the future, long-term interest rates will likely rise. But as goofy as Ben has been, I doubt we get a big enough spike in a short enough time to send 10-year rates from under 2% to above 10% very fast.

So interest rates will rise at some point—which can erode the value of bonds you hold now. Some investors may say, "Yes, but I'll hold my bonds to maturity." Fine, you can think that, but 10 years is a long time. Thirty years much longer! And if you must sell, even a small interest rate move can seriously impact your return. Exhibit 3.2 shows the impact of rising interest

Exhibit 3.2   Interest Rate Risk

		Current 10-Year Treasury Issue US Treasury 1.6% 8/15/22 Current YTM 1.8%		Current 30-Year Treasury Issue US Treasury 2.8% 8/15/42 Current YTM 3.0%	
		Projected Yield	Implied Total Return in 1 Year	Projected Yield	Implied Total Return in 1 Year
	400	5.8%	−55.5%	7.0%	−97.5%
	300	4.8%	−43.1%	6.0%	−80.6%
	200	3.8%	−29.5%	5.0%	−59.2%
	100	2.8%	−14.6%	4.0%	−32.0%
Potential Change in Yield-to-Maturity	50	2.3%	−6.6%	3.5%	−15.6%
	0	1.8%	1.8%	3.0%	3.0%
	−50	1.3%	10.6%	2.5%	24.1%
	−100	0.8%	19.9%	2.0%	48.1%
	−200	−0.2%	39.8%	1.0%	106.7%

Source: Bloomberg Finance L.P., as of 10/25/2012.

rates on the value of 10-year and 30-year bonds. A 1% upward rate move wouldn't be unusual in a year—that gives you an implied −14.6% annual return on your 10-year Treasury—not what you think bonds do. A 2% move is pretty big, but again, if interest rates are rising, some volatility wouldn't be unusual. That would be an implied −29.5% return on the 10-year or −59.2% on the 30-year. The more interest rates rise, the worse the total return. That's interest rate risk—don't ignore it.

Portfolio Risk and Food Risk

There's inflation risk, political risk, exchange rate risk, liquidity risk. On and on and on. Volatility is decidedly not the only risk investors face.

In 1997, I wrote a paper on risk with my friend and sometimes research collaborator Meir Statman (the Glenn Klimek Professor of Finance at Santa Clara University's Leavey School of Business) titled, "The Mean-Variance-Optimization Puzzle: Security Portfolios and Food Portfolios," published in the *Financial Analysts Journal*.

Our research shows that the way people think about food and investing often parallels. In food, folks want multiple things at the same time. They don't just want nutrition—they want food to look good and taste good. And they want to eat food at the right time of day. Cereal is a breakfast food—eating it at night is just sad. And diners want prestige! Packaging matters.

What folks want from food can shift, fast. And what they feel as risk is what they want at a point in time that they think (or fear) they're not getting. They don't think about the things they are getting. For example: Maybe they're forced to eat cereal at night— nothing else in the house. They don't like that they're eating something in the wrong order, and they feel foolish for it. Won't admit it at work the next day! Those are two risks. They don't think about the need that's being fulfilled, i.e., basic sustenance.

How does that relate to investing? As with dining, what folks feel as risk is often that which investors aren't getting at a point in time—never mind if their other objectives are being met. You might hear investors say something like, "I don't want any downside volatility!" They're feeling volatility and want protection from it. Then, if stocks go on a long, sustained tear, they might feel like they're missing out—and *missing out* is felt as another kind of risk.

When Opportunity Doesn't Knock

That risk is called *opportunity cost*—the risk of taking or failing to take actions now that results in lower returns than you would have gotten otherwise. And it can be a killer.

For example, you may have a longer investing time horizon, but perhaps you're mostly concerned about shorter-term volatility and not any other form of risk. You may then choose to have too large a permanent allocation of fixed income than would otherwise be appropriate for your long-term objectives. Over your longer time horizon, because you don't have enough exposure to equities, you likely get lower returns and increase the likelihood you miss your long-term objectives—maybe by a wide margin.

That can hurt—a lot. Particularly if you're depending on your portfolio to provide cash flow in retirement. If you're planning on a certain level of cash flow, but your portfolio suffers from opportunity cost over a long period, you may find you must ratchet back your spending.

What makes opportunity cost such a killer is its deleterious impact may not be obvious for some time. You may have a 20- or 30-year time horizon—or more! Twenty years from now, if you look back and discover you really needed to annualize 9% or 10% on average, but your lower short-term volatility portfolio yielded much less, that's a massive portfolio error that may simply be beyond help. Twenty years of too-low returns is hard (if not impossible) to make up—particularly if you're now taking cash flow. To reduce the odds you run out of money too soon, you may have to cut your spending. And that can be hard to do, even dispiriting, if you've been counting on a larger income—particularly if you're already retired or nearing retirement—more so if your spouse was also counting on that income. That's tough enough to take, and tougher still to explain to your spouse.

And yet, most investors probably don't think much about opportunity cost. Not normally. It tends to pop up as a broad concern after a bull market has been running for a while and usually coincides with extreme optimism or even euphoria. For example, in late 1999 and 2000, suddenly, investors everywhere were keen to chase the next big thing. The big returns of the 1990s made big equity returns seem easy—too easy. They wanted to ratchet risk—buy all hot Technology stocks! Oh, no! The opportunity cost of not day-trading hot recent Tech IPOs! And you know how that played out.

But typically, investors default to focusing most on volatility and less (or not at all) on opportunity cost. Why is this very real risk often given second-class status? Warren Buffett popularized the saying, "You should be greedy when others are fearful and fearful when others are greedy." Recall, for complex reasons rooted deep in the way our brains evolved over millennia, we tend to be hard-wired to fear losses more than we enjoy the prospect of gain. (See Chapter 1.) And by and large, investors tend to disbelieve bull markets as they run.

Which is perverse! And yet, most readers of this book will agree that, overall and on average, investors tend to be bullish when they should be bearish and the reverse. So if stocks rise something on the order of 72% of all calendar years, folks are just going to be naturally bearish more often than not—and they're going to downplay opportunity cost as a risk.

Don't do it. Volatility is a key risk, but not the only one. For many investors with long time horizons, not accepting *enough* volatility—opportunity risk—can be more devastating long term.

Chapter Four

More Volatile
Than Ever

~

*"Stocks are just more
volatile now."*

SOUND LIKE SOMETHING you've heard? Or read? Or believe to be true?

Investors don't just tend to focus mostly on shorter-term volatility (Chapter 3). They often fear volatility is increasing! And it may *feel* true. We had a big bear market in 2008—the biggest since the Great Depression. Soon after, there was a big global correction in 2010 on eurozone-implosion fears. And another big correction in 2011 and a smaller though still scary correction in 2012. Many posit the onset of high-frequency trading and speculators have contributed to increasing levels of stock volatility.

Don't believe it—it's a myth.

First, volatility is itself volatile. It's normal to go through periods of higher and lower volatility. Second, it's a fallacy to assume higher volatility spells trouble. Third—volatility in recent years (as I write) isn't all that unusual and is well within normal historical ranges.

Volatility Goes Up, Too

Pop quiz: Which year was more volatile? 2008 or 2009?

Most investors will automatically know US and global stocks fell huge in 2008 and then boomed huge in 2009. But they may wrongly assume stocks were more volatile in 2008.

Not so. As measured by standard deviation (a widely used metric for volatility), 2008's standard deviation was 20.1% and 2009's was 21.3%.[1] (Measured using US stocks, which I use throughout this chapter for their longer history.) Yes! 2009 was *more* volatile!

How can it be? To understand that, you must understand a few things about standard deviation. *Standard deviation* is just what it sounds like—a measure of how much something deviates from its average. It can be used to measure historical volatility of single stocks, sectors, the market as a whole, anything for which you have enough data points—sunny days in San Francisco, rainy days in Portland. A low standard deviation means results didn't vary much from the average. A higher standard deviation means there was more variability.

As of year-end 2011, the S&P 500's annualized standard deviation since 1926 was 15.6%.[2] (That's based on monthly returns. You can measure standard deviation with yearly returns, but you get fewer data points. You can measure with daily returns as well, but I'm not sure why you'd want to, and the industry mostly uses monthly.) But that includes the steeply volatile years of the two Great Depression bear markets, which drag the average up a bit. Since 1926, median standard deviation was 13.0%. (See Exhibit 4.1.) So both 2008 and 2009 were well above the median, and one year was terrible, the other terrific.

It's also important to remember standard deviation is inherently backward looking. It's a useful tool but tells you nothing about how volatile or unvolatile anything will be immediately ahead. It describes how stocks behaved in the past on average. Like all historical data, it's a useful guide—it gives you a range of what's reasonable to expect. But volatility is never a forecasting tool.

Exhibit 4.1   Volatility Is Volatile—and Normal

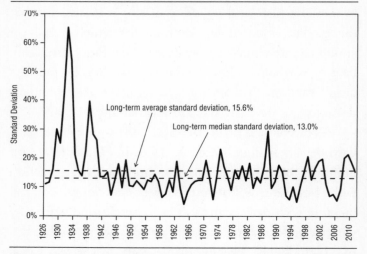

Average and median standard deviation are calculated using the average annual standard deviation as of 12/31 of each year.

Sources: Global Financial Data, Inc., as of 9/20/12, S&P 500 Total Return Index from 12/31/1925 to 12/31/2011.[3]

A standard deviation of 0 tells you, historically, returns have never varied—like cash stuffed in your mattress (ignoring inflation's eroding impact over time). You don't need historical standard deviation to tell you stocks have been pretty darn volatile. I bring it up because, again, stock market volatility is itself volatile. Some years, market volatility is vastly above average. Some years, it's vastly below average. And some years, both happen! The front is hugely volatile, and the back isn't, and vice versa.

An average is an average and bakes in huge variability around it.

What's more, stocks can rise and fall on both above- and below-average volatility. There's no predictive pattern.

Volatility Isn't Predictive

The most volatile year ever was 1932—standard deviation was 65.4%.[4] But stocks were down just –8.9% for the year. Not great, but not the disaster most would naturally expect from monster volatility. All that tells you is within the year, monthly returns were wildly variable—as you'd expect in the final year of the first down-leg of the Great Depression.

The second most volatile year ever was 1933. Standard deviation was 52.9%—but stocks rose a massive 53.9%.[5] That starts to make sense when you get in your bones what volatility is (how much something deviates from its average) and what volatility isn't (a bad thing that measures only stock market downside).

Big volatility doesn't mean stocks must fall. In 1998, standard deviation was 20.6%. Way above average, yet stocks were up 28.6%.[6] In 2010, standard deviation was 18.4% and stocks rose 15.1%.[7] In 1980, standard deviation was 17.4% and stocks boomed 32.3%.[8]

Yes, big volatility has happened in down years. But not always and not enough to make you automatically fear above-average volatility. And the reverse is true. Lower volatility doesn't automatically mean big returns. In 1977, standard deviation was a below-average 9.0% and stocks fell –7.4%—returns nearly identical to 1932's return but with much less volatility.[9] Standard deviation was 9.2% in 1953 and stocks fell –1.1%.[10] Standard deviation was a low 7.6% in 2005, and stock returns were also low—just 4.9%.[11]

When standard deviation is around its long-term median (from 12% to 14%) returns also vary hugely. In 1951, standard deviation was 12.1% and US stocks boomed 24.6%.[12] In 1973, standard deviation was 13.7%, and US stocks fell –14.8%.[13]

There is nothing about any level of volatility that is predictive. Rather, standard deviation is descriptive of the past—and the past doesn't dictate the future.

Volatility Is Volatile—And Not Trending Higher

So volatility isn't predictive. But it isn't trending higher, either. Folks may remember the Flash Crash in May 2010, when within mere minutes, broad markets plummeted. Stocks were down nearly 10% at one point intraday, only to quickly reverse most of that mid-day fall (while still ending the day down). The crash was broadly blamed on a string of technical glitches. Many blamed the proliferation of high-frequency trading (HFT), not just for the Flash Crash, but for increasing volatility overall.

But where's the proof volatility is increasing? Look back at Exhibit 4.1. Sure, volatility was higher in 2008, 2009 and 2010, but it fell off a bit again in 2011. That higher volatility wasn't out of line with past peaks. And it's not trending higher—it's just the same variability of volatility we've seen through history.

And if you fear high frequency trading increases volatility, know it existed in 2003, 2004, 2005, 2006 and 2007—when standard deviation was relatively lower. Folks used computers to trade in 1987 when standard deviation hit a peak, but they weren't doing anything like today's HFT. Nobody thought of HFT at all in 1974, 1970, 1962 or any other earlier peak volatility period.

See it another way: The Great Depression was wildly volatile—both up and down. Folks tend to think of the Great Depression as one long period of stagnation, but it wasn't. It was two recessions with a growth interval between and two huge bear markets with a huge bull market between—history's second biggest.

Volatility then had myriad causes. One was a relative lack of liquidity and transparency. There just weren't as many stocks then, nor as many transactions and many fewer market participants. Information moved more slowly, so price discovery was tough. Spreads between bid and ask prices for all but the very largest stocks were much greater as a percentage of the total price then, so the bounce between someone hitting the bid or pushing on the ask moved transaction prices a wider percent of the total price. Put all that together and you get much more volatility, regardless of other macro drivers (like disastrous monetary policy, fiscal missteps, insanely ill-gotten trade policy, a lousy economy, massive uncertainty, Hitler's rise, Huey Long and a whole lot more).

Similarly, thinly traded markets even today are generally more volatile—like penny stocks, micro-cap stocks (frequently the same thing) or very small Emerging Markets countries. Because there are vastly more publicly traded stocks now, vastly more participants and information is easily and instantly available, markets *should* be inherently *less* volatile overall than the thinly traded Great Depression days. I'm not saying you'll wake up next week and stocks will behave like bonds. No! And you don't want them to if you want them to deliver long-term superior returns. Rather, we're less prone to get the intensely wild swings we saw then and still see today in thinly traded markets.

Hug a Speculator

Another popular, much-maligned scapegoat for increased volatility (whether or not that increased volatility is actually happening) is speculators.

Speculators aren't *bad*. In fact—if you buy a stock, you are, in a sense, a speculator! Even if you hold it for a long period—a year or 10 or 50—when you buy a stock or sell it short, you speculate it's going to do something. There's nothing wrong with that.

But that's not what folks usually mean when they talk about *speculators*—they're typically referring to futures traders. A futures contract is an agreement to buy or sell something at an agreed-upon price at a future date—a commodity, a stock index, interest or exchange rate, whatever. Effectively, it's a bet on future price direction. Often, speculators never take possession of the thing whose price they're betting on. Maybe they don't even *want* to! They're purely speculating on future price movement and don't want or need the soybeans, pork bellies, currencies, whatever. This is particularly egregious to those who fear speculators.

When oil prices rise sharply, it's near guaranteed media headlines will blame speculators—folks messing with the rest of us just to make a quick buck. But they don't realize: Speculators don't just bet prices will rise; they often bet prices will fall. And because speculators, as a group, don't work together, some will speculate prices will rise at the exact time others speculate prices will fall. Speculators aren't some financial geniuses who only win at our expense. They can and do lose money—just like any investor.

Then, too, when prices fall, you (usually) don't hear folks blaming speculators for that—though speculators are probably as responsible for downward spikes as they are for upward spikes (i.e., not very).

Plus, there are myriad legitimate reasons to trade futures. Businesses use them all the time to smooth input costs on volatile commodities. Airlines often buy fuel futures to smooth those costs for travelers, and you probably like your airline ticket prices to not swing wildly. Farmers buy futures! They need feed grain, fertilizer, fuel and other commodities, and their profit margins can be hugely impacted by sharp price swings—and commodities are prone to sharp swings. When you think "futures trader" it probably doesn't conjure an image of *American Gothic*—but maybe it should.

But futures contracts—and those speculators—play an important role in capital markets. They increase liquidity. They also increase transparency and speed price discovery—also good things. Folks often overlook the benefit of increased liquidity—but again, the mere fact there are more transactions happening can actually reduce volatility.

We can prove this—with onions. In 1958, onion farmers convinced Michigan Congressman (and later President) Gerald Ford speculators were wreaking havoc in onion markets and depressing prices. He sponsored a bill that became law (and remains law to this day) banning speculation in onions.

Was it all sunshine and happiness for onions thereafter? Not really. If you think oil is volatile, you've never looked at onion prices. Exhibit 4.2 shows onion prices and oil prices—just by eyeballing it, you can tell onions have much huger and more frequent boom/busts. (Hat tip: Mark J. Perry and John Stossel.)

Exhibit 4.2   Volatility and Onions

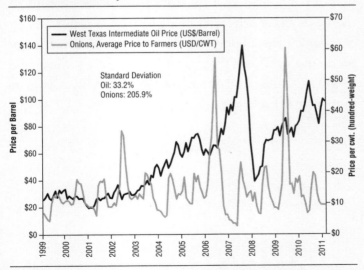

Source: Global Financial Data, Inc., as of 09/25/12, West Texas Intermediate Oil Price (US$/Barrel) and Onions, Average Price to Farmers (USD/CWT) from 12/31/1999 to 12/31/2011.

Don't just trust your eyes. You can measure standard deviation as well. Standard deviation for oil from 2000 through year-end 2011 was 33.2%, but for onions it was 205.9%!

Remember that the next time someone says the cure to the market's ills is banning speculators. Such a move wouldn't necessarily reduce volatility, and it may well increase it—along with reducing transparency and slowing price discovery. (Politicians cannot and will not ever understand how free markets work. I'm convinced it's a virus that destroys part of their brains in the 12 to 24 months after being elected to major office.) So thank a speculator, and don't fear volatility. It's not predictive, you can't get upside volatility without the downside, and over time, upside volatility happens more often. Embrace it.

Chapter Five

The Holy Grail—
Capital Preservation
and Growth

~

*"You can have capital
preservation and growth
at the same time!"*

IF SOMEONE OFFERED YOU a "capital preservation and growth" strategy, would you take it? Sounds pretty good. Who doesn't want all the benefit of equity-like upside growth with downside capital protection? Both at the same darn time!

And who doesn't want to eat rib-eyes and ice cream sundaes every night but never gain weight?

The idea you can pursue capital preservation *and* growth at the same time as a unified goal is no different than the notion of a low-cal, fat-free, guilt-free rib-eye-and-sundae dinner. It's a fairytale.

Capital Preservation Requires *No* Volatility ...

First, let's clear up common misperceptions about capital preservation. It's a goal likely appropriate for fewer people than you think. And if you think it's something you want (or need) long term, ask yourself why. True capital preservation means your portfolio's absolute value should never fall.

And to do that—true capital preservation—you must eliminate most all volatility risk. (As discussed in Chapter 3, volatility isn't the only risk investors must consider.) But if you eliminate volatility risk, you not only avoid the times stocks are down, you avoid the 72% of all years stocks are up! Effectively, you're limited to cash or near-cash vehicles, which means likely seeing purchasing power eroded over time by inflation.

Sure, you could get better-than-cash returns by investing in Treasurys. But if you do that correctly, you're giving up some flexibility. How so? Treasurys can and do experience price volatility and have had shorter periods of negative returns. (Again, see Chapter 3.) Which means if you sell a Treasury prior to maturity, you can sell at a loss. (Yes, that's the opposite of a capital preservation strategy.) So to accomplish capital preservation via Treasurys, you likely must hold them to maturity.

But that's *still* a strategy that may lag inflation. Inflation's long-term average is 3%.[1] As I write, the 10-year Treasury rate is 1.6%.[2] The 30-year rate is 2.8%![3] If you lock up your funds for 30 years, you might *just* lag inflation. And if you don't hold to maturity, again, you can sell at a loss. And with interest rates at historic lows, odds are they do rise in the long period ahead, diminishing the value of your bond portfolio.

That's capital preservation—the absence of volatility risk. Which means true capital preservation is rarely appropriate for investors with long time horizons.

... But Growth Requires Volatility!

On the other hand, growth—even mild growth— *requires* some volatility risk. It's the opposite of capital preservation. I can't say it enough: Without downside volatility, there is no upside. And as shown in Chapter 1, upside volatility happens more often (72% of all years) and to a bigger degree, even if our brains don't remember it that way.

Which means, as a unified goal, you simply cannot have capital preservation and growth at the same time. It would be a physical impossibility. *You cannot have upside volatility with no downside volatility*. If someone tells you otherwise, they're lying to you. Maybe unintentionally, which is bad. Maybe intentionally, which is worse! The more growth appropriate for you, the more shorter-term volatility you should expect. No way around that. Accept that now, and your expectations won't be out of whack. (Out-of-whack expectations can be very damaging indeed—see Chapter 17.)

And yes, steep shorter-term volatility can be difficult to experience—a reason many investors fall short of their long-term goals and in-and-out at all the wrong times.

Let me seemingly reverse myself for a moment. You can't have capital preservation and growth as a single, combined goal. However, as a *result* of a long-term growth goal, you very likely will have preserved capital over the long term ahead.

As shown in Chapter 1, over 20-year rolling periods, stocks have never been negative (and they nearly always beat bonds by a wide margin). The past is never a guarantee of the future, but it does tell you if something is reasonable to expect. Human nature hasn't changed enough and won't change enough in your lifetime (or your children's or their children's or for many millennia) to diminish the power of profit motive. As such, it's very likely stocks continue to net superior returns over very long periods ahead.

Which means it's very likely, over the next 20 years, your well-diversified equity portfolio will have grown—maybe a lot. Maybe doubled two or three times or thereabouts. So you will have gotten growth *and* preserved your initial capital with volatility along the way.

Yes, you would have experienced shorter periods of negative returns. And yes, at points, your portfolio may have dropped below your starting value. But over longer periods, the odds are stacked heavily in your favor you will experience growth, which means you've also preserved capital. But that is all the *result* of having a growth goal. If you pursue capital preservation as a goal, after 20 years, you likely have your starting value and not much more.

Which means anyone selling you capital preservation and growth *as a single, combined goal* either doesn't know much about finance theory or is trying to fool you. Either one is bad.

Chapter Six

The GDP–Stock Mismatch Crash

~

"Stocks must crash because they outpace GDP!"

EVERY NOW AND THEN, some talking head will bluster that stock returns are unsustainable and must crash because they far outpace the US economy's growth rate.

It's true! Long term, US GDP real growth has averaged about 3%. But US stocks have appreciated at an annualized 10% average.[1] That's a major gap betwixt.

And if you believe (as many do), over time, the two rates should roughly match, then you may fear the margin between represents some sort of phantom returns. If our country's output grows about 3% a year on average, then where the heck is that excess return coming from?

Viewed that (incorrect) way, that gap is worrisome. Stocks would have to crash a long way to close that long-term annualized gap. Yikes!

Except stock returns and the GDP growth rate aren't linked. They don't match because they shouldn't match. Stocks can, should and probably will continue annualizing a materially higher rate of return than GDP growth. And that makes sense, if you think about what GDP is and what stocks are.

GDP Measures Output, Not Economic Health

GDP is an attempt to measure national output—a wonky and imperfect one at that. It's built on surveys and assumptions and is often restated—even years later. It doesn't measure national assets or national wealth and doesn't try to. Rather, it's a standard economic flow.

See it this way: As of year-end 2011, America's GDP was about $15.3 trillion (in today's dollars).[2] If full-year 2012 GDP growth were 0% (unlikely), America's GDP would be ... still about $15.3 trillion. If America's growth were utterly flat for five years (which would be unlikely and weird), America would have still put $76.5 trillion of output into the world at the end of those five years.

And though many people believe it to be so, GDP isn't perfectly reflective of economic health. Its headline number is calculated thusly:

$$\text{GDP} = \text{Private consumption} + \text{Gross investment} \\ + \text{Government spending} + \text{Net exports} \\ (\text{Exports} - \text{Imports})$$

Gross investment is non-residential investment (you can think of that as business spending) plus residential investment plus change in inventories.

Because GDP measures *net exports* and the US is and has been a net importer for decades, we constantly get dinged on this. Importing more than you export detracts from output but isn't necessarily bad. It can be seen as a sign of economic health! Major developed nations that are net importers (like the US and UK) tend to have higher annualized growth rates than net exporters (like Japan and Germany). And shrinking imports isn't a good thing. If imports fell radically relative to exports, that would actually add to headline GDP. But it's probably a sign of graver problems, like demand collapsing in a recession.

Then, too, many of the goods we import are intermediary goods. They get combined with goods manufactured here, there and everywhere. Then, they're resold here or abroad (contributing, by the way, to headline GDP). And when US firms that imagine a product, then package, market and sell it, can import cheaper inputs, that improves profit margins, adding to shareholder value (which we'll get to in a bit). Oh, and it allows US consumers to buy higher quality goods at cheaper prices. But GDP bean-counters can't capture that benefit.

Shrinking Government Spending Is Good, Not Bad

Then, shrinking government spending *detracts* from GDP. (One reason US GDP wasn't gangbusters in 2011 and into 2012 was shrinking government spending!) But shrinking government spending isn't necessarily a negative. Taking a longer view, it can be a positive!

Consider the so-called PIIGS nations: Portugal, Italy, Ireland, Greece and Spain. Set Ireland aside for a moment—its economy is and has been structurally competitive, and its debt woes were mostly tied to its troubled banks, which the government bailed out. But for the remaining PIGS, decades of bloated government spending have crowded out the private sector—the degree of crowding out varies among nations. The private sector is a supremely smarter and more efficient spender of capital than any government—so their economies are much less competitive than much of core Europe. After all, when a business spends money, that capital comes from profit or a loan. If that spending doesn't result in higher profits later, the business eventually ceases to be. That's creative destruction, and it's a powerful force for societal good.

But the government isn't subject to the forces of creative destruction. When the government spends money, first, it seizes it from you and me. That's money, now, you and I cannot spend smartly on stuff we want or need. Or it's money we can't spend starting a new business. Or it's money a business can't spend researching cool new products or upgrading equipment or hiring or ... or ... or ... So the government takes money out of the hands of private individuals and firms who spend it wisely pursuing their own self-interests. Then it fusses around with it a bit and spends it on something of dubious value.

If the government spends money badly (as it often does) ... it doesn't go out of business. And if it needs more money later, it doesn't have to create something of value that generates profits. It just taxes us more later! (Any private firm that operated that way would be out of business before I could finish typing this sentence.)

If politicians spend money *really* badly, maybe some of them lose their jobs in the next election. But they just get replaced with more politicians who, again, aren't held to remotely the same fiscal accountability as you or I or private firms are. If politicians spend money *really, really* badly, maybe they become Chairman of the Ways and Means Committee.

So, for example, when many argue the PIIGS nations have *too much debt* and that's the root cause of their problems, they have it wrong. No—there's no level of debt inherently right or wrong or proven reliably problematic. (See Chapter 13.) The problem with those nations is decades of too much government.

Too Far, Too Fast?

Which brings us to stocks. But bear with me for another moment before we get into what stocks are, and let's clear up another misperception. A variation on this GDP–stock mismatch theme is that stocks have risen too far, too fast—and what goes up must fall. Typically, folks making this argument cite a chart looking something like Exhibit 6.1, which shows S&P 500 total returns over time.

Exhibit 6.1 US Stock Returns, Linear—Looks Are Deceptive

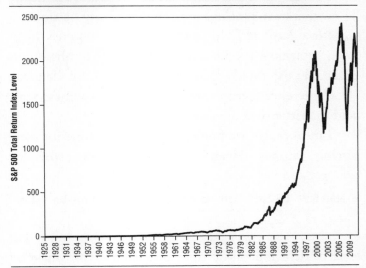

Source: Global Financial Data, Inc., as of 09/24/2012, S&P 500 Total Return Index from 12/31/1925 to 12/31/2011,[3] graphed on a linear scale.

It looks like, through history, stocks had pretty steady returns. Then starting in the mid-1980s or so, stocks took off. Then getting into the late 1990s, things got super-crazy unsustainable. And then we had two big, bear markets—massive looking on this chart— which may only confirm the worst fears of those believing stocks have come "too far, too fast."

First, think about those two bear markets. They were the two biggest since the Great Depression. Now look at 1929 on the chart. Barely a blip! Weird. You already know that wasn't reality, and something may be afoot.

Now look at Exhibit 6.2, which also shows long-term returns. But this chart isn't at all top-heavy or scary. Yet the data in Exhibits 6.1 and 6.2 are identical. The difference is the former is graphed on a linear scale and the latter on a logarithmic scale.

Linear scales are fine and used all the time for measuring returns. Even for stocks they're fine for

Exhibit 6.2   US Stock Returns, Logarithmic—Looks Are Deceptive

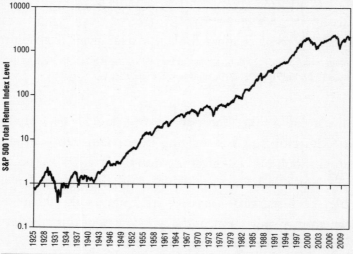

Source: Global Financial Data, Inc., as of 09/24/2012, S&P 500 Total Return Index from 12/31/1925 to 12/31/2011,[4] graphed on a logarithmic scale.

shorter periods. The problem using a linear scale over longer periods when measuring something that compounds is every point move takes up the same amount of vertical space.

On a linear scale, a move from 1,000 to 1,100 looks huge, but a move from 100 to 110 looks tiny. Yet that's not reality. Both are 10% moves and should look the same! Because of the impact of compounding returns over nearly 100 years, on a linear graph, later returns start looking stratospheric because the index level itself is higher.

A logarithmic scale mitigates that and is a better way to consider long-term market returns. On a logarithmic scale, percent changes look the same even if absolute price changes are vastly different—a move from 100 to 200 looks the same as 1,000 to 2,000—both 100% increases. That's how you and your portfolio experience market changes.

What Are Stocks?

As discussed in Chapter 1, stocks are a piece of firm ownership, not a slice of current or future domestic economic output. When you buy a stock, you own a slice of a company and its future earnings, which you expect to rise over time—otherwise you wouldn't buy the stock.

Exhibit 6.3 shows S&P 500 earnings per share over time overlaid with S&P 500 price returns. Not always or perfectly, but they track pretty closely. And they should! But earnings aren't calculated in GDP. Corporate *spending* is, but not earnings.

Sure, one firm's spending may contribute to another firm's earnings. And a firm's earnings may be influenced by whether an economy is growing or not and how strongly. But earnings are a function of revenues minus

Exhibit 6.3   S&P Versus Earnings per Share

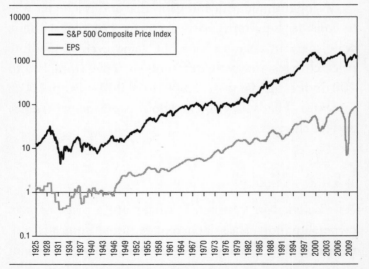

Source: Global Financial Data, Inc., as of 09/24/12; S&P 500 Price Index from 12/31/1925 to 12/31/2011.

costs—and headline GDP has no direct connective tissue to either.

Public firms, i.e., stocks, function in our economy. But the stock market and the economy aren't the same, and they aren't remotely interchangeable. Rates of headline GDP growth and stock returns aren't directly linked and shouldn't be. Earnings, and therefore, stock prices, can and likely will keep growing faster than GDP over time—in the US and globally. Because stocks represent the non-stop exponential upward sweep of the collision of innovations, contributing to higher earnings over time. You can't capture that in an economic flow.

Chapter Seven

10% Forever!

"If stocks return 10%, I can just forever skim 10% off the top."

THERE ARE SOME WHO DOUBT stocks can continue delivering superior returns over time. Those folks should have greater faith in capitalism and/or should revisit Chapter 1.

But then, there are those who believe in the long-term superiority of stocks. Absolutely! Stocks should average 10% a year from here until eternity. Their faith is so sure, they believe they can skim 10% off the top—easy, peasy—every year.

I share their optimism, to a point. I'm not blindly convinced stocks *must* average 10% annually in the long period ahead. My guess is they easily beat bonds over long periods and by a wide margin, and long-term returns are likely to be near the 10% historic average but could easily be a bit more or a bit less. But planning to skim 10% a year is a recipe for total disaster: It ignores the huge variability of returns.

Stock Returns Are Superior—And Variable

As discussed in Chapter 1 and elsewhere, the variability of stocks' short-term returns is one reason stocks have superior long-term averages. We all would *love* stock returns to be steadier (read more in Chapter 17), but that's not reality.

Exhibit 7.1 shows S&P 500 annual return ranges and frequency. The most common result by a plurality (37.2% of all years) is years when stocks finish up huge—over 20%. Next, stocks are most commonly up between 0% and 20%—but *rarely* are they near 10% on the nose.

Some folks have a hard time with this, but disaster years are quite rare—stocks are "down a lot" just 7.0% of all years. Rare! The down years just loom larger in our memories.

Exhibit 7.1   Average Returns Aren't Normal—Normal Returns Are Extreme

S&P 500 Annual Return Range			Occurrences Since 1926	Frequency	
	>	40%	5	5.8%	
30%	to	40%	13	15.1%	Up a lot
20%	to	30%	14	16.3%	(37.2% of the time)
10%	to	20%	17	19.8%	Up a little
0%	to	10%	13	15.1%	(34.9% of the time)
−10%	to	0%	12	14.0%	Down a little
−20%	to	−10%	6	7.0%	(20.9% of the time)
−30%	to	−20%	3	3.5%	
−40%	to	−30%	2	2.3%	Down a lot
	<	−40%	1	1.2%	(7.0% of the time)
Total Occurrences			86		
Simple Average			11.7%		
Annualized Average			9.7%		

Source: Global Financial Data, Inc., as of 07/10/2012, S&P 500 Total Return Index[1] from 12/31/1925 to 12/31/2011.

You can put yourself in a serious hole if you take 10% at a near-term market low—like when stocks are in a big bear market or even down during a briefer (but very common) correction. This may not matter if you have a very short time horizon. But most readers of this book likely have a much longer one—20 years or more. Maybe much more!

Some may say, "Fine, I just won't have a portfolio that falls that much." Ok. You can do that, likely by reducing shorter-term volatility by always having a big allocation of fixed income. However, then you reduce your expected return as well. A portfolio like that probably annualizes much less than 10% over long periods.

Others may decide to just take gains. In a year when stocks rise 25% (as can happen)—*woo hoo!*—take the gains, and it's party time. And stocks do rise more than fall! But what do you do in a year stocks fall 20%, 30% or more as can happen in a bear market? Do you not take cash flows? Do you *add more* cash to get back to your arbitrary line in the sand?

Say you have a $1 million portfolio that falls to $800,000—a normal, short-term move to be expected in an all-equity portfolio. Do you wait until the portfolio reaches $1 million before you take cash flows again? Or does $800,000 become your new baseline? Most folks can't (or don't want to) live with so much cash flow variability.

I See 5% CDs

An alternate version of this: Folks may say, "I'll just forever buy CDs and/or bonds yielding 5%, and that will be a safe way to always have 5% income, forever. No need to touch principal!" Theoretically, if you need $50,000 a year and have a $1 million portfolio, you just keep buying 5% CDs and/or bonds.

Sounds good, but that won't work, either. First, in 2012, 5% CDs are mythical creatures. There are none! Five-year CDs pay under 2%. The best 10-year rate I could find was 2.1%.[2] You know from Chapter 3, 10-year and 30-year Treasurys are yielding 1.6% and 2.8%—*below* inflation's long-term average![3]

Corporate bonds aren't much better. A firm with a pristine credit rating (which doesn't guarantee against future default) pays a 2.1% rate.[4] To get higher yields, you must go junk—rates are 6.6% for 10-year bonds as I write.[5] And that's *junk*! If you're relying on a CD and/or bond strategy for reliable cash flow, a strategy heavily exposed to junk bonds may not be appropriate. Sure, you can buy junk to increase expected return, but if you're going that route, 6.6% is pretty darn low. Depending on your goals and time horizon, it might make more sense to trade the increased default risk in junk bonds for higher volatility risk in stocks. Long-term returns are likely better with stocks.

So, via your CD-strategy, as I write, your $1 million portfolio doesn't kick off $50,000 but instead likely around $21,000 in a 10-year CD.

Yes, interest rates are historically low—for CDs, bonds, etc. Eventually, at some future point, they'll rise. Maybe you think you'll just sell what you have now to buy the higher yielding instruments later.

But don't forget: Yield and price have an inverse relationship. As rates rise, the prices of your bonds fall—if you sell, you can sell at a loss. And there are usually penalties if you sell CDs before they mature. Now you're working from a lower portfolio value. Probably not what you had in mind.

Or you could wait it out so you don't lose principal and just buy higher-yielding instruments as your current ones mature. Fair enough! But while you wait, you likely must accept lower cash flow until then. And who knows how long it will take for 5-year CD rates to go from under 2% to over 5%. Maybe they don't—not for a long, long time.

And even then, *don't forget inflation*. If you need $50,000 in today's dollars, in 10 years, you'll likely need over $67,000 just to maintain status quo purchasing power if inflation is anything like the long-term average in the period ahead. In 20 years you'll need over $90,000! (See Chapter 2.)

Hey, maybe interest rates rise really far, really fast—and one day, you *can* buy a CD yielding 9%! That would solve your purchasing power problem, wouldn't it?

Probably not. That $90,000 after 20 years assumes inflation is about average over the period ahead. In a world where CDs pay 9% (and not fake ones like the ones convicted Ponzi scammer Sir R. Allen Stanford sold—see Chapter 17), inflation has probably risen a lot, too, and seriously taken a whack out of your purchasing power. Which means that hypothetical future $90,000 may not be enough.

So how should you get income from a portfolio? Read on to Chapter 8.

Meanwhile, in my view, a wiser long-term strategy is determining the totality of your goals and selecting an appropriate benchmark and long-term asset allocation that increases the likelihood you achieve them. (For guidance on how to do that, read my 2012 book, *Plan Your Prosperity*.) And one consideration should be whether that benchmark can sustain your inflation-adjusted cash flows over your long time horizon. The 10% strategy and the 5%-CD-forever plan are both unsustainable myths.

Chapter Eight

High Dividends for Sure Income

~

"To ensure retirement income, I'll just invest in high-dividend stocks."

LONGEVITY KEEPS INCREASING—and only will continue in the future. (See Chapter 2.) Which means folks are likely to spend longer in retirement now than ever—maybe much longer than most anticipated. Getting enough cash flow to fund retirement is often a top concern for many investors.

No one wants surprises in retirement—particularly not the sort of surprise that requires a sudden spending downshift. So how can you increase the odds your portfolio kicks off a level of cash flow you expect for the totality of your time horizon?

A near-ubiquitous myth is funding retirement is easy and predictable with a portfolio heavy in high dividend-yielding stocks and/or fixed income with high coupon rates. Whatever that yield is (so goes the belief) you can safely spend—maybe without ever touching principal! Many investors—including professionals—believe this is a safe (there's that word again) retirement strategy.

Don't count on it. This myth could cause potentially very costly errors. Ones that can force you to ratchet down your future spending—and make for awkward conversations with your spouse.

There are a few problems with the high-dividend myth. First and most simply, this confuses *income* with *cash flow*. Yes, dividends (interest payments, too) are technically *income*. You report them as such on your tax returns. And there's nothing wrong with either as cash flow sources—dividend-paying stocks and fixed income may well be appropriate for you to some varying degree, depending on your long-term goals and financial profile. I can't tell you how much is appropriate for you because I don't know you. But if you rely on them solely or primarily, you could be selling yourself vastly short.

Finance theory is clear: After taxes, you should be agnostic about the source of your cash flow. It doesn't matter whether you get cash flow from dividends, a coupon or the sale of a security. Cash is cash is cash! Instead, what should concern you most is remaining optimally invested based on a benchmark (i.e., long-term asset allocation) appropriate for you. And a portfolio full of high-dividend stocks may not do it. Why?

All major categories of stocks come in and out of favor—including high-dividend stocks. Value and growth trade leadership, as do small cap and big cap. All major sectors rotate—Energy, Tech, Financials, Materials, etc.—going through periods they lead and periods they lag, always and irregularly. And high-dividend stocks are just another equity category. They aren't better performing or less volatile. Sometimes they do well, sometimes they do middling and sometimes they do dreadfully. (More on this in Chapter 9.)

Some investors believe with their very souls a dividend is a sign a firm is healthy. And shouldn't you want a portfolio of just healthy stocks? But there's nothing inherently better about a firm that pays a dividend—it's just a different way of generating shareholder value.

Some firms choose to generate shareholder value by reinvesting profits. They may believe investing in new capital equipment or research or buying (or merging with) a competitor or complementary business will make investors bid up the value of their stock. Other firms may decide reinvestment won't yield much additional growth (either because of where they are in a market cycle or because of the nature of the firms' business or some other reason). So they may generate shareholder value by paying dividends. You see this as a shareholder. When a firm pays a dividend, the share price falls by about the amount of the dividend, all else being equal. After all, the firm is giving away a valuable asset—cash.

Because high dividend-paying firms tend to see more value in giving shareholders cash rather than reinvesting profits, there is some overlap in high-dividend categories and *value* stocks. Whereas growthier firms tend to pay low or no dividends (generally—this isn't a hard-and-fast rule). In general, when value is in favor, high dividend-paying stocks are, too. And when growth outperforms value, high-dividends similarly underperform.

Let me say that again: Value isn't a permanently better category—it trades leadership with growth. *No one category leads for all time* (which we discuss more in Chapter 9).

No Guarantees!

So high-dividend stocks aren't permanently better and don't have materially different expected volatility or return characteristics over time. As important: Dividends aren't guaranteed. Firms that pay them can and do and will cut the dividend. Or they may kill it altogether! PG&E, a utility with a long history of paying dividends, stopped for four years while its stock fell from the low $30s to around $5 between 2001 and 2002. Banks (and plenty of other firms) slashed their dividends during the 2008 credit crisis.

Another myth is the mere existence of a dividend is a testimony to the health of a firm. If a firm pays a dividend, it must be awash in cash and very healthy, right? And the bigger the dividend yield, the healthier the firm must be, right?

Nope. While PG&E experienced its aforementioned price fall, its dividend yield *rose*—but because dividend yield is a function of past payments and current stock prices. A higher dividend then was just a symptom of a falling stock price (and then PG&E suspended the dividend altogether). Now-defunct Lehman Brothers paid a dividend in August 2008— just weeks before imploding. Dividends don't signal sure safety.

What about bond interest? If you rely wholly or partially on interest from bonds, you might end up with a too-large fixed income allocation that isn't appropriate for you, which could impact the likelihood you achieve your goals over the long term.

Then, you can't forget about interest rate risk—as discussed in Chapter 3. What happens when you have a 10-year bond paying a 5% coupon maturing in 2012, and a recently issued bond, similar in all ways—term, risk profile, etc.—yields just 1.6%? As I write in 2012, bond yields are and have been historically low. Unless you buy junk-rated bonds (increasing your portfolio risk, which may or may not be appropriate), you probably aren't getting much yield.

There's nothing wrong with getting cash flow from dividends or bonds, but you shouldn't assume they're risk free. And you shouldn't be shackled to them only.

Homegrown Dividends

So if you need cash flow from your portfolio, and you don't want to be stuck in an inappropriately large allocation of high-dividend stocks and/or fixed income, what can you do? You don't want to sell securities, do you?

Sure! Why not? That's what they are there for!

I call this tactic *homegrown dividends*. The term is mine, and it just means harvesting your portfolio however appropriate while remaining optimally invested.

And to do that, you can sell securities. You can! Folks often say, "But I don't want to sell principal." But buying and selling individual securities is incredibly cheap—there's little impediment to keeping your portfolio optimally invested based on your benchmark and selling securities now and then to raise cash.

Raising homegrown dividends also lets you do some tax planning, if appropriate. You can sell securities at a loss, if you like, to offset some gains. Some years you might not be able to do that, but even so, selling stocks with a long-term capital gain results in a relatively small tax liability. And maybe you have loss carry-forwards to mitigate some of that.

And a well-diversified portfolio will likely always include some dividend-paying stocks, so you'll likely still have some cash flow from dividends. But you needn't be hamstrung by just those with higher yields. And depending on your goals and time horizon, you may have some bonds kicking off coupon payments— but depending on your benchmark, that may not be a requirement.

Whether in retirement, approaching retirement or 40 years out, investors should care more about total return—i.e., price appreciation plus dividends—rather than just dividend yield. That allows you to pick a benchmark based on your goals and time horizon, not just on a dividend yield. Focusing solely on dividend yield can mean badly lagging what you would have gotten otherwise as high-dividend stocks go out of favor or watching dividends periodically shrink or get cut. Not a great strategy.

Chapter Nine

The Perma-Superiority of Small-Cap Value

❧

"Small-cap value stocks are just better than other stocks."

THIS IS A MYTH MANY professional investors and hard-core enthusiasts tend to fall for—the belief that small-cap value is inherently better and prone to long-term superiority moving forward, forever and ever, world without end, Amen.

It's not true. Were it, we'd all know it, and everyone would invest in small-cap value, only. But there are also hard-and-fast (equally misguided) adherents to other equity size/style/categories. Some folks only buy large growth. Others buy only Tech. Only US. Only blue chips. Only British mid-cap Pharmaceuticals. Only this. Only that. Name a category, and there's a fan group that believes it's found the long-term silver bullet—its beloved category is best, no analysis needed beyond that. Yet no matter the depth of their love for [insert category here], they can't all be right. And in fact, none are.

Perma-Love or Heat Chasing?

Another big feature of this perma-love: Often, it isn't so permanent. Yes, some small-value disciples rigidly and adamantly hang on, even during the (sometimes, excruciatingly long) periods small value underperforms, so firm is their faith. But there are some who, after watching a category go on a tear for some time (large growth in the mid- to late-1990s, Tech in the late 1990s, Financials in the mid-2000s, foreign in the 1980s, US for all of the 1990s, Emerging Markets in the late 2000s, etc., etc., etc.), think, "*Aha! This* is the best category! I am missing out. But no more! I am convinced this category is best and will now shift heavily to it." And they often shift in time for leadership to rotate (as it always does, irregularly), and they end up badly lagging. Maybe that hot sector crashes and they get crushed! And maybe they decide they were wrong (again) and go buy another category they see has been leading for some time and believe *that's* the one that's perma-better. This is pure heat chasing, nothing else.

But they don't think they're chasing heat. No! We all know chasing heat is bad. Rather, they think they're being rational. That the recent lengthy outperformance of Category X is evidence it's *just better*. And sure, a particular equity category can outperform for a long time. But that doesn't mean it's permanently superior. It just means sentiment on that category was particularly strong, fundamentals justified its outperformance for a time or a combination of the two. But just because something has led for a long time doesn't mean it must lead for a long time ahead.

As an example, since 1926, small-cap stocks have annualized 11.9% to the S&P 500's 9.9%.[1] Proof small cap is perma-better? Not really. A lot of that outperformance ignores huge bid–ask spreads common in small-cap stocks in the 1930s and 1940s—sometimes up to 30% of the purchase price. If you actually bought and sold small-cap stocks then, costs ate up a major chunk of your return—but that's not captured in long-term index returns.

Then, too, small stocks tend to bounce huge off bear markets—the bigger the bear, the bigger the bounce. But that's relatively short-lived. And small caps bounce huge because they fall huge in the later stages of the bear market—much more than the broad market. If you're waiting for a huge small-cap bounce, you must also live through the huge small-cap plunge—super-emotionally tough. Outside just a few of the relatively hugest small-cap bounce periods, large caps overall beat small caps—and typically for agonizingly long periods. It can be mentally and emotionally trying investing in an asset style for which the relative payoffs are few and far between.

And if you could perfectly time those bounces off bear market bottoms (hard to do), there are myriad other ways to make huge returns that beat small cap then. But those times when big stocks beat small are long enough to drive even the most patient investor absolutely insane. Most of the longest bull markets in history were dominated by big stocks.

Capitalism Basics

Fact is, to believe a category is permanently and inherently better, you must disavow basic tenets of capitalism—primarily, that prices are set by constantly moving forces of supply and demand. In a basic college economics class, this probably was described to you as eagerness. How emotionally eager are consumers to buy (i.e., demand) something at varying prices? At higher prices, generally (but not always), consumers want less of something than at lower prices.

Supply is about eagerness, too. How eager are suppliers to produce more or less of something at varying prices? Typically (but not always), producers will be more eager to produce something at a higher price than at a lower. At a point, consumer eagerness and producer eagerness meet—that's your price. A price is an amazing technology. Folks don't think about it that way, but a price is a simple manifestation of thousands, maybe millions, maybe billions of factors all colliding at a point where a buyer will buy and a seller will sell. (Politicians are forever wanting to tinker with prices, but that's because politicians aren't capitalists and cannot and will not ever understand the capital markets pricing mechanism.)

Why did I say "but not always" twice? Sometimes, consumers *do* want something more at a higher price. The higher price might be part of the emotional package, tied to prestige or perceived quality or some other thing the buyer values. When Apple produces a next-generation iPhone, for example, some folks wait in line to get the product the first day, even though the product is no different in three months and in six months, the price likely drops hugely. And sometimes, technological advances reduce costs for producers, making them more eager to produce at a lower price. (Basically, that's

Moore's Law in action.) Still, this is all a reflection of varying levels of eagerness to consume or produce.

Though media and pundits try to tie stock price movements to every imaginable factor, when you boil them down, stock prices, like everything else we buy in free markets, are driven by supply and demand.

Near term, stock supply is relatively fixed. Initial public offerings (IPOs) and new stock issuances take tremendous time, effort and regulatory input—and they get announced well ahead of time. Cash- and debt-based mergers and share buybacks reduce supply but are also typically telegraphed ahead of time. Bankruptcies can also reduce supply but don't happen in large enough volume to move the stock supply needle much. So over the next 12 to 24 months, you tend not to get big, unexpected stock supply swings. That's when demand rules, driven largely by fickle sentiment—getting more positive or negative—which can happen fast.

But longer term, supply pressures swamp all else. Stock supply can expand or shrink near endlessly over the long term in perfectly unpredictable patterns—increasing through issuances or shrinking through buybacks and cash- or debt-based takeovers.

What happens is, one category starts getting more interest—like Tech in the late 1990s. Entrepreneurs and venture capitalists note that increasing demand and see investors willing to bid up values of that category—money seems easy to raise. They want in on that and the future profitability they think they can generate on relatively easy money. At the same time, investment bankers, whose societal purpose is to help firms access capital markets, also see growing demand in Category X. They help entrepreneurs by issuing new shares or new debt to raise money to launch a firm. Done right, this is profitable for all involved.

Or maybe it's not a new firm. It's an existing firm that doesn't want to miss out on potential profits from hot Category X. So it, too, issues shares or debt to raise money to start a new division or maybe buy another firm with expertise in that area. Or maybe it just wants capital to buy new equipment or do research or development. Business owners are happy to do this because they envision big future profits from their activity. Investors are happy to buy the shares because they want a piece of those future profits. And investment bankers are happy to help firms issue shares or debt because, again, it can be profitable for them. (Never forget the powerful force for societal good profit motive is.)

The investment bankers keep printing new stock for new and established firms until, ultimately, supply swamps demand, and prices fall.

Sometimes prices fall slowly, sometimes quickly—but demand falls and investment bankers don't want to issue shares for the cold category as much anymore. They want to issue shares for the next hot (or even warm) category—increasing stock supply there. Meanwhile, excess supply in the now-cold category can get swept up as corporations buy back shares or go bankrupt or get swallowed by other firms. Supply can expand and contract endlessly and, in the long term, will overcome any major demand shifts.

And because firms will always be motivated to raise capital at different points, and because investment bankers will always be motivated to help firms who need (or want) to raise capital by issuing shares to meet demand (or manage buybacks and takeovers for firms), future supply will always be unpredictable, but overpowering, in the longer term.

Demand should float from category to category irregularly. There's no fundamental reason why, 10 years from now, investment bankers should want to issue more shares of Tech versus Energy versus a larger category like small-cap or large. Each category—if well constructed—should travel its own path but net very similar returns over über-long periods, as the forces of supply ultimately drive long-term returns.

Another way to think about that is Exhibit 9.1, which looks like a crazy mish-mash quilt with no discernible pattern. It shows major asset classes (large-cap

Exhibit 9.1 No One Style Is Best for All Time

Performance ranking of investment styles by year (best to worst):

1992: Russell 2000 Value 29.1% · S&P/Citi Value 9.5% · Russell 2000 Growth 7.8% · S&P 500 Index 7.6% · Barclays Agg 7.4% · S&P/Citi Growth 4.6% · MSCI EAFE −12.2%

1993: MSCI EAFE 32.6% · Russell 2000 Value 23.8% · S&P/Citi Value 16.6% · Russell 2000 Growth 13.4% · S&P 500 Index 10.1% · Barclays Agg 9.8% · S&P/Citi Growth 0.2%

1994: MSCI EAFE 7.8% · S&P/Citi Growth 3.1% · S&P 500 Index 1.3% · S&P/Citi Value −0.6% · Russell 2000 Value −1.5% · Russell 2000 Growth −2.4% · Barclays Agg −2.9%

1995: S&P/Citi Growth 39.4% · S&P 500 Index 37.6% · S&P/Citi Value 37.2% · Russell 2000 Growth 31.0% · Russell 2000 Value 25.7% · Barclays Agg 18.5% · MSCI EAFE 11.2%

1996: S&P/Citi Growth 23.7% · S&P/Citi Value 23.6% · S&P 500 Index 23.0% · Russell 2000 Value 21.4% · Russell 2000 Growth 11.3% · MSCI EAFE 6.0% · Barclays Agg 3.6%

1997: S&P/Citi Growth 33.5% · S&P 500 Index 33.4% · S&P/Citi Value 33.3% · Russell 2000 Value 31.8% · Russell 2000 Growth 12.9% · Barclays Agg 9.7% · MSCI EAFE 1.8%

1998: S&P/Citi Growth 41.0% · S&P 500 Index 28.6% · MSCI EAFE 20.0% · S&P/Citi Value 18.2% · Barclays Agg 8.7% · Russell 2000 Growth 1.2% · Russell 2000 Value −6.5%

1999: Russell 2000 Growth 43.1% · S&P/Citi Growth 35.9% · MSCI EAFE 27.0% · S&P 500 Index 21.0% · S&P/Citi Value 4.7% · Barclays Agg −0.8% · Russell 2000 Value −1.5%

2000: Russell 2000 Value 22.8% · Barclays Agg 11.6% · S&P/Citi Value −6.9% · S&P 500 Index −9.1% · MSCI EAFE −14.2% · S&P/Citi Growth −22.3% · Russell 2000 Growth −22.4%

2001: Russell 2000 Value 14.0% · Barclays Agg 8.4% · Russell 2000 Growth −9.2% · S&P/Citi Value −9.4% · S&P/Citi Growth −10.9% · S&P 500 Index −11.9% · MSCI EAFE −21.4%

2002: Barclays Agg 10.3% · Russell 2000 Value −11.4% · MSCI EAFE −15.9% · S&P/Citi Value −16.2% · S&P 500 Index −22.1% · S&P/Citi Growth −23.6% · Russell 2000 Growth −30.3%

2003: Russell 2000 Growth 48.5% · Russell 2000 Value 46.0% · MSCI EAFE 38.6% · S&P/Citi Value 31.6% · S&P 500 Index 28.7% · S&P/Citi Growth 26.8% · Barclays Agg 4.1%

2004: Russell 2000 Value 22.2% · MSCI EAFE 20.2% · S&P/Citi Value 15.3% · Russell 2000 Growth 14.3% · S&P 500 Index 10.9% · S&P/Citi Growth 6.3% · Barclays Agg 4.3%

2005: MSCI EAFE 13.5% · S&P/Citi Value 9.2% · S&P 500 Index 4.9% · Russell 2000 Growth 4.7% · Barclays Agg 2.4% · S&P/Citi Growth 2.3%

2006: MSCI EAFE 26.3% · Russell 2000 Value 23.5% · S&P/Citi Value 20.7% · S&P 500 Index 15.8% · Russell 2000 Growth 13.4% · S&P/Citi Growth 11.4% · Barclays Agg 4.3%

2007: MSCI EAFE 11.2% · S&P/Citi Growth 10.3% · Russell 2000 Growth 7.1% · Barclays Agg 7.0% · S&P 500 Index 5.5% · S&P/Citi Value 3.9% · Russell 2000 Value −9.8%

2008: Barclays Agg 5.2% · Russell 2000 Value −28.9% · S&P 500 Index −37.0% · S&P/Citi Growth −38.5% · S&P/Citi Value −38.9% · MSCI EAFE −43.4%

2009: S&P/Citi Growth 34.6% · Russell 2000 Growth 34.5% · MSCI EAFE 31.8% · S&P 500 Index 26.5% · S&P/Citi Value 21.6% · Russell 2000 Value 20.6% · Barclays Agg 5.9%

2010: Russell 2000 Growth 29.1% · Russell 2000 Value 24.5% · S&P 500 Index 15.1% · S&P/Citi Growth 14.1% · MSCI EAFE 7.8% · Barclays Agg 6.6%

2011: Barclays Agg 7.9% · S&P/Citi Growth 2.7% · S&P 500 Index 2.1% · S&P/Citi Value 0.2% · S&P 500 Index −0.7% · Russell 2000 Growth −2.9% · Russell 2000 Value −5.5% · MSCI EAFE −12.1%

Source: Thomson Reuters.[2]

US, large-cap foreign, large US growth, small value, bonds, etc.,) and how they performed each year relative to other categories. So, in 1990, small-cap value did best, and foreign stocks (MSCI EAFE) did worst. The next year, foreign stocks did best! But the boxes move around. Buying last year's winner didn't result in next year's winner, nor did being a contrarian and buying last year's loser. Sometimes one style does best for a while and then gets buried. But no one box dominates, and there's no predictive quality.

Another key takeaway from Exhibit 9.1: If you don't have a fundamental reason for favoring something other than it's been hot, you're probably just chasing heat. That may work for a bit from pure coincidence but isn't a long-term winning strategy. In fact, it's more likely a long-term losing strategy.

Don't fall in perma-love. Love is just another form of bias, blinding you to reality.

Chapter Ten

Wait Until You're Sure

~

"Stocks seem so uncertain now. I'll just wait until they're acting more normally— then I'll make a move."

SOUND FAMILIAR? Have you said or thought that? Or heard someone say it? Plenty of investors think this way—whether it's in the middle of a bear market, a correction or even during a normal bull market run when volatility kicks up a bit.

But what is this normalcy folks are waiting for? A big "GET IN NOW!" sign? Or are they waiting for stocks to stop being so darn volatile and start appreciating in neat, tidy, non-panicky gradual-but-steady steps?

Wait for that, and you'll wait forever. The idea stocks will and should behave "normally" and give you an all-clear buy signal is pure myth. Stocks are normally volatile—sometimes more volatile, sometimes less, but volatile all the same. (Revisit Chapter 4.) And you want them to be. Sounds perverse, but it's true. Finance theory is clear: You can't get much return without risk (i.e., volatility). If stocks had lower shorter-term volatility characteristics, the returns would be lower over time. If you want better returns, you must accept a higher level of shorter-term volatility. If you want lower shorter-term volatility, you should expect lower returns.

But this idea investors should wait until things seem more clear tends to pop up more frequently in the steep, painful bottoming period of a bear market—those days when stocks can swing wildly—maybe 4%, 5%, 6% or more in a single day! Yikes.

Then, it can feel like waiting a bit until things are clearer—until *you're sure* the bear market is over and the new bull under way—is a smart move. Maybe you're already invested—stayed with the market throughout the bear. But the late bear market vicissitudes are wearing on you—and you're scared there's more to come. Should you bail, wait out the end and then get back in when the signs are clearer? (Another question: Are you that good a market timer? If so, why didn't you time the top?)

Or maybe you're out and know you should get back in. But when? If you're out, deciding to get back in can be incredibly hard—maybe harder than deciding to get out. Is it better to wait until it's certain the bear market is over?

No—clarity is one of the most expensive things to purchase in capital markets. That's true whether it's a bull, bear or any of the innumerable countertrend rallies within. And as counterintuitive as it seems, risk is actually least just when fear is highest and sentiment is most black—right as a bear market is bottoming. Clarity is almost always an illusion—a very expensive one.

No one can perfectly time bear market bottoms. Sure, you can get lucky! But luck isn't a strategy—it's an accident. As painful as late bear market wild wiggles are in the shorter term, you don't want to miss the start of a new bull market. New bull market returns are super-swift and massive—quickly erasing almost all late-stage downside volatility. Even if you suffer the last 15% to 20% of a bear market, it's still almost certainly small compared to the subsequent initial up-leg of the next bull market.

TGH at Work

Exhibit 10.1 shows how a typical bear market works—like a spring. The more you depress it, the bigger the bounce. Sure, bear markets can (and often do) double-bottom, but that doesn't diminish the bounce. And given enough time, W-bottoms resolve into more of a V.

When a bear market starts, deteriorating fundamentals drive the initial drop. Folks think bear markets start with a bang—they usually don't. Corrections start like that—a big, sentiment-driven drop that

Exhibit 10.1   Hypothetical V-Bounce

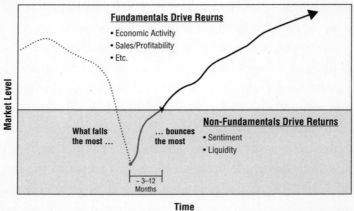

Note: For illustrative purposes only. Not drawn to scale. Not to be interpreted as a forecast.

scares the pants off most everyone. It would be much easier if bear markets had that pants-off scaring announcement factor. "Hey! Big bear coming!" But the reason so many people get ensnared is bull market tops tend to roll over, and the new bear slowly grinds lower. It doesn't look or feel like a bear market—it feels like sideways choppiness, which happens during the course of bull markets, too!

I call the stock market "The Great Humiliator" (TGH)—its aim is to humiliate as many people as it can for as long as it can for as many dollars as it can. And a favorite trick of TGH is to fool folks into a false sense of security with a rolling bull-market top. A sudden big-bang effect would make it too easy for folks to see a bear forming and get out with minimal humiliation.

It's the latter portion where the bang happens. At a point, diminishing liquidity (like we saw in the fall of 2008 during the financial crisis) and sentiment take over from fundamentals. Panic often ensues.

But panic is usually just sentiment and the temporary lack of liquidity that goes with the sentiment shift and is often confused with something fundamental. Stock valuations often become detached from reality. Which is why timing bear market bottoms is so devilishly tough. Sentiment is hard to gauge with any form of accuracy, anyway. And sentiment moves fast. Which is

why, as a new bull market starts, the right side of the
V-bottom can happen just as fast.

The V-Bounce

Folks often disbelieve new bull markets—often for
years after they begin. But particularly in the early stages.
"How can it be a bull market when everything is so
bad?" they wonder.

And everything probably *is* pretty bad. Bull markets
often start before economic contractions bottom. But
stocks don't boom because things are improving. Rather,
they boom because everyone expects Armageddon, but
at a point, Armageddon doesn't happen, and folks realize reality isn't so dire. The panic was overdone. Just
that slight sentiment melt on hugely depressed valuations can make stocks take off like a bullet. And the
shape of the initial stage of the new bull market typically
about matches the speed and shape of the end of the
bear—what I call the "V-bounce" effect.

(Another common V characteristic: In the late
stages of a bear, when sentiment is driving big volatility,
those categories that fall most tend to bounce most
in the early part of the new bull. Read more on that in
Chapter 19 of my 2010 book, *Debunkery*.)

It's not just theory—we see the V through history.
Exhibits 10.2 through 10.5 show some of history's

Exhibit 10.2   A Real V-Bounce—1942

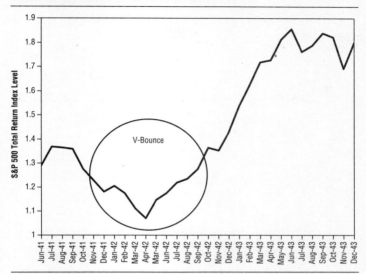

Source: Global Financial Data, Inc., as of 10/25/2012, S&P 500 Total Return Index (monthly data) from 06/30/1941 to 12/31/1943.[1]

V-bounces. Sometimes, bear markets end in more of a double-bottom W—with both bottoms a few months apart. And it can seem for a very short time like a W—but with minimal time, it resolves into a basic V pattern—and the bottom of the W portion begins to look tiny by comparison.

Missing those huge, early V-bounce returns while waiting for some illusory sense of "clarity" can mean

Exhibit 10.3   A Real V-Bounce—1974

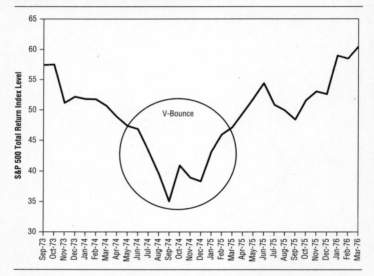

Source: Global Financial Data, Inc., as of 10/25/2012, S&P 500 Total Return Index (monthly data) from 09/30/1973 to 3/31/1976.[2]

missing your chance to erase a big portion of your prior bear market losses. And it also hurts you relative to your benchmark. The ancestral part of our brains says, "Yikes! We fell a lot! Let's protect ourselves so we can't fall more!" If we act on that, it can make us feel better immediately—for a short while. But it can rob us of the huge returns we normally get from the early bull

Exhibit 10.4   A Real V-Bounce—2002

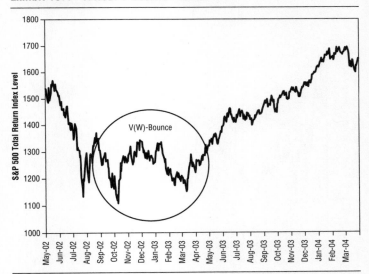

Source: Global Financial Data, Inc., as of 10/25/2012, S&P 500 Total Return Index (daily data) from 05/31/2002 to 3/31/2004.[3]

V-bounce. They may not undo all of the bear market, but they certainly put you on the way.

Volatility is huge on *both* sides of the V bottom. It's only in retrospect you know which volatility you're suffering through—late bear or early bull. But if you miss those early returns, you will regret it. Exhibit 10.6 shows how massive those early returns can be—averaging

Exhibit 10.5   A Real V-Bounce—2009

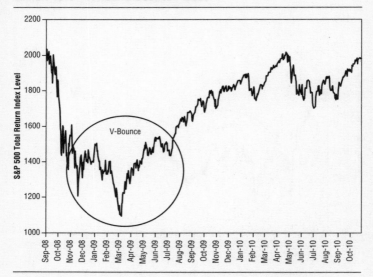

Source: Global Financial Data, Inc., as of 10/25/2012, S&P 500 Total Return Index (monthly data) from 09/30/2008 to 10/31/2010.[4]

21.8% in the first 3 months and 44.8% in the first 12 months! What's more, the first 12 months are consistently big and fast—obviously some bigger and faster than others, but all big and fast nonetheless. A bull market's average annual return is 21%[5]—but a bull market's average first year more than *doubles* that!

And almost half those first-year returns usually (but not always) come in the first three months! And here,

Exhibit 10.6   First 3 and 12 Months of a New Bull Market—S&P 500

Bull Market Start	Bull Market End	First 3 Months' Return	First 12 Months' Return
06/01/1932	03/06/1937	92.3%	120.9%
04/28/1942	05/29/1946	15.4%	53.7%
06/13/1949	08/02/1956	16.2%	42.0%
10/22/1957	12/12/1961	5.7%	31.0%
06/26/1962	02/09/1966	7.3%	32.7%
10/07/1966	11/29/1968	12.3%	32.9%
05/26/1970	01/11/1973	17.2%	43.7%
10/03/1974	11/28/1980	13.5%	38.0%
08/12/1982	08/25/1987	36.2%	58.3%
12/04/1987	07/16/1990	19.4%	21.4%
10/11/1990	03/24/2000	6.7%	29.1%
10/09/2002	10/09/2007	19.4%	33.7%
03/09/2009	????	39.3%	68.6%
Average		**21.8%**	**44.8%**

Source: Global Financial Data, Inc., as of 10/25/2012, S&P 500 Price Index average is calculated for all bull market periods ending 10/09/2007.

too, the market is tricky. Because on the occasions when the first three months aren't so straight up, folks are prone to think it's a sign the big boom will never come. This is just the market head-faking folks in another of its standard TGH humiliation tactics. Sometimes when the bottom is choppy on the left side of the V, it is also choppy on the right side, discouraging investors. But the V pretty much always works over a year.

Most all bull markets start this way—you can see it in history. Yet instead of a V (or W), people are usually instead looking for the agonizingly long-term L-shape. But I challenge them to find three examples of that ever in developed markets' history. Only the onset of World War II in Europe knocked a global bull market off-course into a legitimate dragged-out L. A nascent bull market kicked off in 1938 but was truncated soon after the Nazis invaded the Sudetenland in 1939. Stocks didn't finally bottom until 1942—and then surged in earnest.

If you believe stocks won't boom off the bottom, you better have a darned good reason to expect it. Only the threat of Nazis taking over the world with a communist Soviet overhang was enough to ever prevent a legitimate V-bounce. And all it really did was delay it—after the 1942 bottom, stocks formed the right side of the V. Stocks are resilient. That's no myth.

Chapter Eleven

Stop-Losses
Stop Losses

~

"A stop-loss can stop your losses!"

EVEN THE *name* stop-loss sounds good. Who doesn't want to stop losses? Except, stop-losses don't do what people want them to. Instead, they tend to trigger taxable events and more transaction fees. And they more often stop gains than they do losses—on average over the long-term, they're a money loser. Don't buy into this costly myth.

Stop-losses come and go in popularity. You tend not to hear much about them in the latter stages of a bull market. Sir John Templeton famously said, "Bull markets are born in pessimism, grow on skepticism, mature on optimism and die of euphoria." Stop-losses are mostly a pessimism–skepticism game, though they have adherents no matter the market cycle. They tend to appeal to people who think downside volatility is bad but upside volatility isn't volatility at all. But as discussed in Chapter 4, you can't get the upside without the downside.

The Stop-Loss Mechanics

For the uninitiated, a stop-loss is some mechanical methodology, like an order placed with a broker, to automatically sell a stock (or bond, exchange-traded fund [ETF], mutual fund, the whole market, whatever) when it falls a certain amount.

That amount is up to you! There's no "right" amount for a stop loss (mostly because there's no level proven to improve long-term performance). Typically, folks tend to pick round numbers like 10% or 15% or 20% lower than their purchase price. No reason— people just like round numbers. Nice and neat. They could do 11.385% or 19.4562%, but they don't. No statistical reason why 20% is better than 19.4562%.

The idea is the stop-loss is supposed to protect investors from big downside. If a stock drops and hits the stop-loss level, it's sold. No big 80% drop disasters. Which sounds appealing! Who doesn't want to stop losses?

But they just don't work—not like people hope they do.

If they worked, every professional would use them. If they netted better gains with limited downside, that's a money manager's dream. It would make clients more money. More money for the client is more money for the manager. Win-win-win! Yet, I'm not aware of any major longtime successful money manager who uses them—not even occasionally. I have no doubt some financial salespeople may promote them. Not because they improve performance (because provably, they don't). But stop-losses force sales, and if you're paid by the transaction, using stop-losses is one good way to increase the number of transactions. Good for the sales-person, but a conflict of interest and not optimal for the client.

Stock Prices Aren't Serially Correlated

To believe stop-losses work, you must believe stocks are *serially correlated*. If something is serially correlated, it means past price movements predict future price movements, i.e., a falling stock will keep falling, and a rising stock will keep rising.

There's a school of investing built around this idea, called *momentum investing*. Contrary to a vast body of scholarly research (not to mention actual empirical evidence), these folks believe price movement is predictive. They buy winners and cut losers. They look for patterns in charts. But momentum investors don't do better on average than any other school of investors. In fact, they mostly do worse. Can you name five legendary momentum investors? I can't think of one.

Stop-losses and momentum investing don't work because *stocks aren't serially correlated*. A price's movement yesterday on its own has zero impact on what happens today or tomorrow.

Stocks that fall a certain amount—whether 5%, 7%, 10%, 15%, 19.4562%—aren't more likely to keep falling. Yet stop-lossians act as if that's so. Think it through: Would you only buy stocks that had risen a bunch? Instinctively, you know that wouldn't work. Sometimes a stock that rises a lot keeps rising, sometimes it goes down and sometimes it bounces along sideways. My guess is most people get this in their bones: What goes up doesn't necessarily keep going up. So why don't folks understand that correctly on the downside?

Certainly, stop-losses appeal to that caveman part of our brains that hates losses more intensely than it likes gains (what's known as *myopic loss aversion*). But falling prey to evolutionary responses hurts much more often than it helps in investing. Who wants to invest like a caveman?

Pick a Level, Any Level

Suppose you wanted to do stop-losses anyway, against my recommendation and contrary to the industry-standard investing disclosure that "past performance is not indicative of future results." What level would you pick? And why? Suppose you picked 20%, just because you like the number 20. (It's as good a reason as any other reason to pick a stop-loss level.) When a stock drops beyond that amount, it triggers your stop-loss, and you automatically sell.

But it's basically a 50–50 chance it continues dropping or reverses course. You're trading on a coin flip. Coin flips make bad investment advisers.

For example, the stop-loss won't stop you and say, "Hey, why do you think that stock dropped 20%? Was it because the entire market corrected that much, and your stock went along for the ride?" Market corrections are common—happen about once every year. If a stock drops with the broader market, that's not necessarily the stock's fault. The stop-loss then doesn't protect you against loss; it just guarantees you sold at a relative low and paid another transaction fee. You might be sitting in cash when the market—and your now-sold stock—reverse course fast and zoom to fresh highs. This is buying high, selling low.

And what do you buy next? Maybe the next stock you buy also eventually drops 20%, triggering another stop-loss. Repeat. Repeat. You can buy 20% losers (or 10% or 19.4562%) all the way to zero. Just because you use a stop-loss doesn't guarantee your next purchase will only rise. And maybe the initial stock you automatically sold reversed course and zoomed up over 80% in the next year. You missed that! You sold at a relative low, paid two transaction fees and missed out on the good part. Maybe you tell yourself you'll buy back once you think the trouble has passed, but I say, "Nonsense." If you sold automatically, what fundamentals are you looking at to tell you to buy back in? And if you could somehow know with certainty when trouble had passed, you wouldn't need a stop-loss at all. In fact, you'd probably already be unimaginably rich and wouldn't need this book.

Here's another way to see this. Suppose you buy XYZ stock at $50 and it zooms to $100. Then your friend Bob buys it, and it drops to $80—down 20%. Should you both sell? Or just him with his higher cost basis? For him the stock is down 20%, but for you, it's still up 60%. Does that mean the stock is ok for you, but not ok for him? Why?

That's the problem with stop-losses. There's no answer to "Why?" other than, "Just because." *Just because* isn't a strategy.

Stop-losses don't guarantee protection against losses. They do increase the odds you miss out on upside, and they definitely increase transaction costs—perhaps why some brokers have never stopped promoting them. There's no evidence they produce better results, but there's mountains of evidence to the contrary. Better to think of them by the name that describes them better: stop-gains. Stop yourself before using stop-losses.

Chapter Twelve

High Unemployment Kills Stocks

~

"High unemployment is an economic and stock market drag."

THIS MYTH—and it is decidedly and eminently provably a myth—is about as ingrained an economic/investing myth as ever existed. It ranks up there with the belief that federal debt is inherently bad (more in Chapter 13) as myths everyone believes—with their souls—no matter their ideology or creed.

Every politician declares high unemployment is bad for the economy—and therefore the stock market. (But it's never their fault! It's always the fault of their opposition.) And politicians are united in their intransigent view that high unemployment *causes* economic weakness.

Yet this is utterly backwards. Unemployment can be excruciating for the unemployed and their families, and we'd all prefer that everyone who wants a job could more easily get one. However, that doesn't change the fact unemployment is now, always has been and always will be a lagging indicator. Said another way: Unemployment, high or low, is the *result* of past economic conditions, not a *cause* of future economic direction. We do not need low unemployment for the economy to grow, and high unemployment will not hinder economic growth going forward. Economic growth drives the need to hire, and a contracting economy drives the need to reduce headcount.

All of this is easy to see if you think like a CEO would and not like a politician wants you to.

See It Like a CEO

Pretend you are CEO of ABC Widgets, Inc. After four or five years of steady earnings growth, your revenues start falling. Slowly at first, so you think you can pull through. You start cutting costs—you tell your employees to telecommute instead of flying to meet new clients. You put off expansion plans. Sales start falling faster, and you cut costs more. Eventually, you recognize sales may not rebound fast. You're not certain an official recession is underway—US recessions are always officially dated (by the National Bureau of Economic Research—NBER) after the fact. But you know what your business is doing, and based on what you hear from suppliers, vendors, etc., you're concerned a prolonged downturn could be underway.

You also realize you've cut costs all you can and now must turn to the last place employers like to cuts costs: employees. You hate doing it, but to keep the firm afloat, you must reduce headcount.

Politicians never understand this, either. Employers hate cutting employees. They don't do it frivolously. But if you don't cut headcount, you could endanger the entire firm—and a bankrupt firm results in many more unemployed people. A firm that survives a downturn is one that can usually start hiring again, eventually.

So you cut headcount. And maybe, after three or four or five tough quarters, your sales do tick up, just a bit. You're well off peak sales volumes, but earnings are going in the right direction, in large part thanks to your cost cutting.

Do you start hiring? No! Not unless you want your board to fire you! First, you don't know if that sales increase was a one-time blip. Plus, your employees are handling your sales volume fine. Maybe better than fine—they've innovated new processes to make their lives easier with the reduced headcount. That's the silver lining to recessions—many firms see huge productivity gains as remaining employees learn to make do with less. And those productivity gains are what let firms see huge earnings growth off even small top-line sales increases.

A few quarters go by—but you still aren't hiring. Revenues are improving but haven't fully recovered. But you are turning a nice profit, which you aren't rushing to spend in the event of that always-feared but rarely seen phenomenon: the double-dip recession. A cash cushion can help smooth out future bumps.

Finally, you become more confident sales are on a sustained upward trajectory. Maybe NBER officially dates the end of the recession a few quarters back. But you still don't rush into hiring full-time labor. Maybe you start with part-time or contract labor—cheaper to hire, easier to fire if things turn around fast. Finally, when you become convinced future sales could be imperiled if you don't materially increase headcount, you start hiring full-time labor in a meaningful way.

Seen this way, it makes sense that unemployment wouldn't fall *before* a recession ends. Rather, it makes sense that unemployment might even rise and/or stay high for some time, even after the economy bottomed and started recovering.

The Economy Leads, Unemployment Lags

It's not just theory. Exhibits 12.1 and 12.2 show historic unemployment rates and recessions. (I've split the historic data in two so you can really see how unemployment moves going into and out of a recession.) Through history, you see unemployment has never fallen before a recession ends. The reverse—it often rises after

Exhibit 12.1   Unemployment and Recessions, 1929 to 1970

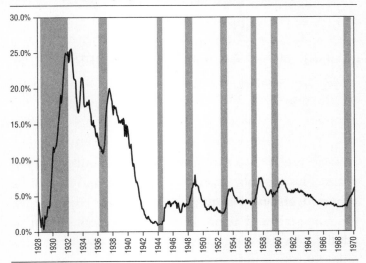

Sources: Global Financial Data, Inc., as of 09/26/2012, Thomson Reuters, US Bureau of Labor Statistics, National Bureau of Economic Research, from 12/31/1928 to 12/31/1970.

Exhibit 12.2   Unemployment and Recessions, 1971 to 2012

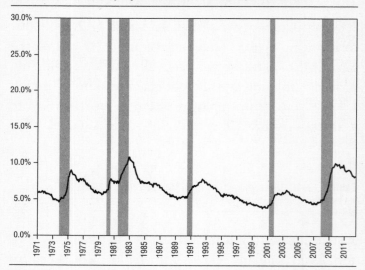

Sources: Thomson Reuters, US Bureau of Labor Statistics, National Bureau of Economic Research, from 12/31/1970 to 06/30/2012.

recessions and then *stays high* for many months or even years. This isn't abnormal—it is normal and should be expected. It would be weird and contrary to economic fundamentals and actual history for unemployment to fall before a recession ends. Yet, politicians and pundits talk as if it should be so!

Pick up any newspaper, and you'd be forgiven for thinking low unemployment *causes* economic growth.

If that were true, low unemployment would be a self-perpetuating growth machine. But that's not the case. Recessions start, always, at or near cyclical unemployment lows. Which isn't what would happen if low unemployment were an economic panacea. Rather, the data prove low unemployment doesn't prevent recessions, and high unemployment doesn't prevent economic growth. Being unemployed can be painful, but no matter the societal impact, that doesn't change the fact economic growth begets lower unemployment, not the other way around.

As an investor, you should care about unemployment's impact (or lack thereof) on the stock market, too. Many similarly fear high unemployment is bad for stocks. But to believe that, you must misunderstand what stocks are and how they behave.

The Stock Market *Really* Leads

The stock market is the ultimate leading indicator for the economy—investors don't wait for economic data to show economic recovery is underway; they bid up stocks ahead of time. So if stocks lead and unemployment lags, there's no way unemployment, high or low, can be a material stock market driver.

Don't take it on faith: Check history. Exhibit 12.3 shows cyclical unemployment peaks and forward

Exhibit 12.3   Unemployment and S&P 500 Returns—Stocks Lead, Jobs Lag

Unemployment Peak	S&P 500 Forward 12-Month Returns	6 Months Before Unemployment Peak	S&P 500 Forward 12-Month Returns
5/31/1933	3.0%	11/30/1932	57.7%
6/30/1938	−1.7%	12/31/1937	33.2%
2/28/1947	−4.3%	8/30/1946	−3.4%
10/31/1949	30.5%	4/30/1949	31.3%
9/30/1954	40.9%	3/31/1954	42.3%
7/31/1958	32.4%	1/31/1958	37.9%
5/31/1961	−7.7%	11/30/1960	32.3%
8/31/1971	15.5%	2/26/1971	13.2%
5/30/1975	14.3%	11/29/1974	36.2%
7/31/1980	12.9%	1/31/1980	19.3%
12/31/1982	22.5%	6/30/1982	61.1%
6/30/1992	13.6%	12/31/1991	7.6%
6/30/2003	19.1%	12/31/2002	28.7%
10/31/2009	16.5%	4/30/2009	38.8%
Average	**14.8%**		**31.2%**

Sources: Bureau of Labor Statistics; Global Financial Data, Inc., as of 09/26/20012, S&P 500 Total Return Index.[1]

12-month stock returns (using the longer history of US stocks). It also shows 12-month returns starting 6 months *before* the unemployment peak—i.e., when unemployment is still rising. Stock returns average 14.8% 12 months after an unemployment peak. Pretty great! But if you bought 6 months before the peak, your subsequent 12-month average return was a big 31.2%. Over double!

Don't take this as a forecasting tool. You couldn't time unemployment peaks (nor the point six months before) if you wanted to. I don't know anyone who's done it or even tried. But what this shows is stocks can and do rise when unemployment is high and rising. There's no evidence high unemployment is a market negative. Just the reverse! Because unemployment is typically high as a recession is ending and just after. And stocks move first—and fast. (See Chapter 10.)

It's amazing this myth persists, particularly since there are ample data to check. So why does it?

First, because folks don't normally check if those things "everyone knows" to be true are actually true. It would be like doubting yourself, which we don't like doing. And it would mean potentially feeling silly for falling prey to a myth—which we *really* don't like doing.

But second, in some ways, it might seem intuitive high unemployment would be economically bad. This is based on the idea consumer demand is a major driver of our economy.

And it is, in a sense. Consumer spending accounts for 71% of GDP, now.[2] But people misunderstand where the bulk of growth is coming from.

If a lot of people are unemployed, that means they have less discretionary income to spend, which, following this logic, should ding the economy and ding stocks.

Right? And yet, since the economy bottomed in 2009, consumer spending has steadily grown in the US and has been above the pre-recession peak level since December 2010.[3] Yet, unemployment is still historically elevated! How can that be?

Consumer Spending Is Incredibly Stable

The truth is, US consumer spending is incredibly stable—it doesn't shrink much in recessions so needn't bounce back much in recoveries. That's because much of what consumers buy is staples and necessary services. When times are tough, we generally still buy toothpaste and prescription drugs. And we spend on services like insurance, housing, utilities, etc. Maybe we switch from the fancy brand toothpaste to the generic, and maybe we're more vigilant about using less heat, switching off lights, etc. But by and large, our average staple spending is pretty darn stable.

Exhibit 12.4 shows the components of private consumption and how much they fell from the peak of real GDP growth in Q1 2008 to the trough in Q2 2009. And it shows how much of total spending each component comprised at the recession's end.

By far, the largest component of consumer spending (67.2%) is on services. During the 2007–2009 recession—which was steep by history's standards—services

Exhibit 12.4   Components of Private Consumption—Services Are Huge and Stable

	Percent of Consumption (Q2 09)	Q1 08 to Q2 09 Real Growth
Gross Domestic Product		**−4.7%**
Personal Consumption Expenditures	**100%**	**−3.4%**
Durable goods	*10.6%*	*−13.1%*
Motor vehicles and parts	3.5%	−21.4%
Furnishings and durable household equipment	2.4%	−13.8%
Recreational goods and vehicles	3.2%	−5.2%
Other durable goods	1.6%	−9.6%
Nondurable goods	*22.2%*	*−3.7%*
Food and beverages purchased for off-premises consumption	7.5%	−3.7%
Clothing and footwear	3.2%	−7.3%
Gasoline and other energy goods	3.3%	−2.9%
Other nondurable goods	8.2%	−2.4%
Services	**67.2%**	**−1.5%**
Household consumption expenditures (for services)	*64.4%*	*−1.8%*
Housing and utilities	18.9%	1.7%
Health care	16.3%	3.4%
Transportation services	2.9%	−13.5%
Recreation services	3.7%	−5.8%
Food services and accommodations	6.1%	−5.7%
Financial services and insurance	7.4%	−8.5%
Other services	9.0%	−3.2%
Final consumption expenditures of nonprofit institutions serving households	*2.8%*	*6.5%*

Source: Bureau of Economic Analysis; percent of consumption based on Q2 2009 GDP "Third Estimate" nominal values, last revised October 26, 2012.

spending fell just –1.5%. Spending actually *increased* on the two biggest services components: housing and utilities, and health care.

The next biggest chunk of consumer spending (22.2%) is on *nondurable goods*. Nondurables are things intended to last less than three years like shoes, clothing and groceries. These tend to be things you need more than you want, and this category fell just –3.7% peak to trough.

Just 10.6% of spending is on *durable goods*. These are mostly (but not exclusively) big-ticket items. They comprise the smallest component, yet they're the headline-grabbing items, i.e., "Auto sales fell 25%!" But is it so shocking that during a downturn, folks would put off buying a car, a washing machine or a flat-screen TV? That's not great for those industries, but it's not economically disastrous, either. Meanwhile, folks generally keep paying for basic necessities. Which is why, during the past few recessions, consumer spending as a percent of GDP has actually risen! (See Exhibit 12.5.)

Yes, consumer spending does tend to fall a bit overall during recessions, but not as much as aggregate GDP. Business spending is a smaller but much more volatile component and is typically responsible for a bigger chunk of GDP's rate change. Exhibit 12.6 shows the peak-to-trough contributors of major components

Exhibit 12.5   Consumer Spending as a Percent of GDP in Recessions Rises

Source: Thomson Reuters, Personal Consumption Expenditures as of 05/15/2012.

of GDP during the 2007–2009 recession. (Though NBER dated the recession as starting in December 2007, output didn't peak until Q1 2008.) Imports added to GDP, as did government spending, a bit.

Residential investment shaved off some output, but probably not nearly as much as most folks would think. Folks wrongly presume a weak housing market was the primary cause of the recession and 2008 credit crisis

Exhibit 12.6   Contributors to US GDP Decline Q1 2008 to Q2 2009

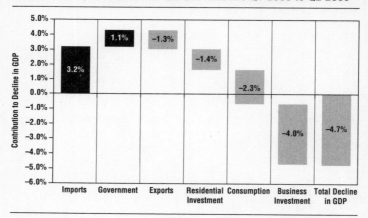

Source: Bureau of Economic Analysis, percentage point contributions peak-to-trough decline in US GDP (Q2 2008 to Q2 2009).

and bear market—but the reality is housing is too small a portion of GDP to have a very big impact. Consumer spending contributed −2.3%—not insignificant, but smaller than the −4.0% contribution from business investment. Had business spending been just flat, that would have been a mild recession indeed.

But, as mentioned, business spending is rarely flat in recessions. Recessions are recessions in large part because of the volatility of business spending. What's more, businesses, i.e., producers, are the true drivers of economic vibrancy. Folks get this backwards, believing consumer demand is king. But if producers don't produce, consumers can't consume.

Producers in the Driver's Seat

This isn't a chicken-versus-egg debate. It's simply the way the world works. If you don't have entrepreneurs risking personal capital on a bet they can produce something the marketplace will like, you don't get very much economic vibrancy.

See it this way. It's 2012 as I write. Just 15 years ago, maybe you had a cellphone, maybe you didn't. Maybe it was a big clunky thing you'd be mortified to be seen with now. Did you know, 15 years later, huge swaths of humanity would be inseparable from their smartphones? That these tiny collisions of technology and consumer electronics would make your life easier? That you would get twitchy if you were separated from yours for more than a couple of hours? No! Someone invented first-generation smartphones—and they seemed like cool playthings for the super-rich and/or gear heads. Then the second generation came around. Then there were myriad copycats as technological advance collided with increased demand and production, driving down costs so they became economical for most anyone. Now they're ubiquitous and being used in ways you never could have imagined 15 years ago. Heck, they're being used in ways the original smartphone producers probably didn't (and couldn't) fathom.

What decidedly did *not* happen was crowds' banging down doors at their local electronics store saying, "Hey! I need a portable phone that's also a computer, calendar and rolodex! It'd better use touch-screen technology, which is a thing no one has really heard of yet! Oh, and it absolutely *must* include a game where you catapult birds at buildings of wood, stone and ice in order to kill baby bird–stealing pigs!"

Had you said such a thing, someone would have had you committed.

No, innovative entrepreneurs, building on past innovations (see Chapter 1), invented smartphones, and the world decided it couldn't live without them. And then cottage industries proliferated to design and deliver apps doing anything and everything you can imagine.

And that's how the economy really works. Without producers' producing—whether they're staples or discretionary goods or services—you don't have much of an economy at all.

Which is why folks get it so backwards when it comes to unemployment and the economy. Consumer demand isn't the volatile driver of economic growth or lack thereof. It's much too stable, even during periods of heightened unemployment. Producers are the major economic growth engines, and they want to take risk to produce something they think will lead to increased profits down the road.

Politicians can rant and rave and wave blaming fingers all they like. But if they want unemployment to be lower, they should pass policies aimed at lowering barriers to entrepreneurship. It's the growth that leads to the need for hiring, not the reverse. Never the reverse.

Chapter Thirteen

Over-Indebted America

~

*"America has too much debt!
And it's a major problem!"*

YOU WON'T FIND ANYONE who disagrees America is over-indebted. Societally, most just accept federal debt is bad—the bigger the debt, the bigger the bad. But remember, those things accepted without question are often those things most needing investigation.

Most people rationally understand that on a personal level, debt is ok. Some people get into trouble, which isn't good. But most understand that debt, managed responsibly, is fine. In fact, necessary! Most folks couldn't buy a house or a car without debt. Heck, most couldn't buy a suit for that first job interview.

Most readers are probably also ok with corporate debt. Again, we understand some firms handle debt badly. But they have a major incentive not to—if they handle it really badly, maybe the CEO gets fired, which he/she doesn't want. Maybe shareholders get mad and dump the stock. Or maybe the company goes bankrupt! All situations rational CEOs want to avoid.

But corporations often use debt to do things like build new factories, finance research or buy competitors or complementary businesses to expand. These things all help firms make or increase profits, and we like profitable companies. Profitable companies give us goods and services we want or need at a reasonable price. And they hire! All good things.

But this rational thinking tends to break down when it comes to government debt. We don't like local government debt, and we detest state government debt, but our fiercest vitriol is reserved for federal debt.

The Government Is a Stupid Spender

Perhaps, rightly, many readers recognize governments are terrible stewards of your money—and the federal government is worse than the state, which is worse than the local government. All true! Governments are indeed very stupid, inefficient spenders of your money. Still, even the most ardent libertarian can agree we need roads and such. And the government establishes and enforces rules and regulations that protect both buyers and sellers, which is good. In my mind, perhaps the most important function of government is the fierce protection of private property rights.

I do wish the government spent less money. Not from any ideological standpoint, but just because I think you would spend it in much smarter ways that would benefit you and your family. And when you spend your money in self-interested ways, that's ultimately better for society. If you don't believe that, then you must not believe in capitalism. And if you don't believe in capitalism, I'm not sure why you're reading a book about stocks. But it was Adam Smith who said, "It is not from the benevolence of the butcher, the brewer or the baker that we expect our dinner, but from their regard to their own interest." Which means, societally, we're overall better off on average if, individually, we do what we view as best for ourselves. And you can do that better if you get to keep more of your money, the government less.

So I wish the government wouldn't be such a stupid spender, but I don't fear its debt—and neither should you. For reasons that follow.

First, people often say the US has "too much debt." But that implies there's some "right" amount of debt governments should have, and there's a hard-and-fast line in the sand that, if crossed, becomes disaster.

Now, many would say the right amount of debt for a government is none. But that's utterly unrealistic. I don't know how a country could issue currency without a debt mechanism, or manage monetary policy. And for those thinking we could return to the gold standard, we still had federal debt when we were previously on the gold standard. What's more, the gold standard didn't protect against any form of economic ill. Bank panics were much more common and severe before the US established the Federal Reserve. The 2007–2009 recession was a walk in the park relative to the huge and frequent depressions of the 19th century.

What's more, some argue a gold (or silver or bi-metallic) standard takes meddling politicians out of monetary policy. This is the exact reverse of what would happen. It takes a huge amount of jiggering to set and then maintain a peg to a hunk of rock—jiggering by politicians. And once the rules are established, politicians can and will change the rules as they see fit. I don't view America's Fed as perfect. Far from it! But metal-based currency invites *more* government intervention, not less. (Nevermind the fact we would have to convince the rest of the world to go to a gold/silver/bi-metallic/

whatever standard, and my guess is many nations would be inclined to tell the US to stuff it.)

Putting Debt in Perspective

But there's no evidence there's a right debt level. What's more, folks fail to put federal debt in perspective, instead citing debt in absolute terms. Exhibit 13.1 shows US net public debt as a percent of GDP, which is the right way to think about it. *Net public debt* is the total debt

Exhibit 13.1   US Net Public Debt as a Percent of GDP

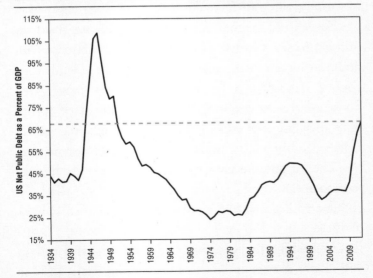

Full-year 2012 data is an estimate.

Source: Office of Management and Budget, US Department of the Treasury, Bureau of Economic Analysis, from 12/31/1933 to 12/31/2012.

held by the public—it doesn't include federal debt held by intra-government agencies, which can be thought of as federal IOUs. After all, when you do your household accounting, you don't consider the 20 bucks you borrowed from your spouse a liability—it's all in the family and in a sense cancels out.

US debt as a percent of GDP is currently elevated—which surprises no one. But it's still well below peak levels. Debt hit 109% of GDP in 1946! But the period that followed isn't remembered as a period of economic ruin. Rather, it's remembered as a period of strong economic expansion and technological advance.

Some would argue it's different now (always a dangerous assumption)—that was war debt. Sure. Except debt doesn't care about the reason it's issued. It's debt! It's a contract. It just has to be paid back, whether it was issued for a noble cause (fighting Nazis) or a silly cause (propping up failing solar panel producers). There's no evidence higher debt then was a proximate cause for economic ruin.

Then again, we have a relatively short data history to examine in the US. But that's not true for the UK. Exhibit 13.2 shows UK debt as a percent of GDP, back to 1700.

Amazingly, the UK has had *much* higher levels of debt. Debt was above 100% of GDP from about 1750 to 1850, above 150% for about half that period and peaked

Exhibit 13.2   UK Net Public Debt as a Percent of GDP

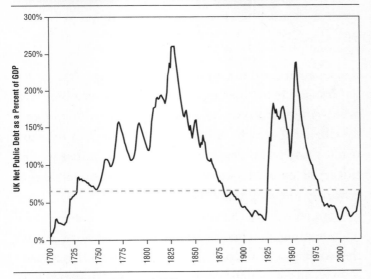

Budget estimations from 2009 through 2012.
Source: HM Treasury, ukpublicspending.co.uk, from 1700 to 2012.

above 250%! Yet, what was going on in the UK in this period and after? Britain was the indisputable global economic and military superpower. The Industrial Revolution kicked off—earlier than in the US. The UK was the center for revolutionary manufacturing practices worldwide. All while it had major levels of debt.

And this was when news traveled by foot, horse, carrier pigeon and only much later by train. If the UK could survive as a superpower with debt above 100%

for a century, there's no reason America's currently elevated debt must be long-term debilitating.

Question Everything!

This may be hard for some readers to accept. Maybe the hardest myth in this book. Indeed, of everything I've ever written, this is the toughest concept for folks to get. The belief that debt is bad is so ingrained in us, most readers may just outright reject what I say, refuse to consider the data or contemplate the fundamentals—or they may just skip this chapter.

But why? Questioning what you believe—even if it's something you deeply believe—doesn't hurt. What's the worst that can happen? You either find out you were right all along, which is fine. Or you find out you believe something that's wrong that's making you see the world all wrong and potentially leading to investing mistakes. Which is great! Because if you can see the world more clearly, you can make fewer mistakes and see greater long-term success. It's win-win either way.

Now, many readers will also say, "But what about Greece? Don't Greece's big debt problems prove debt is bad?" No. It does prove socialism is bad. Greece doesn't have a debt problem—it has a structurally uncompetitive economy thanks to decades of entrenched socialism. And it has a structurally corrupt government (thanks to the socialism) that makes it difficult to reform its ways to help make the economy more competitive going forward.

But Greece's problem wasn't the debt. Its problem was it had been cooking the books and got discovered. That, coupled with its uncompetitive economy, caused debt buyers to demand higher rates. They thought Greece wasn't such a great credit risk anymore. And those higher rates made Greece's debt interest payments very expensive.

The Real Issue ... Affordability

And that's the crux of the problem. The issue isn't debt, but whether that debt is affordable. And America's debt is very affordable. Historically so! Exhibit 13.3 shows federal debt interest payments as a percent of GDP. Though our aggregate debt is higher now, our interest rates are very low—making the debt cheap.

As I write, debt interest costs are lower than the entirety of 1979 to 2001—not a period remembered for economic ruin. The reverse! For much of the 1980s and 1990s, the US was the dominant economic powerhouse. And the 1980s and 1990s featured two mega, near decade-long bull markets. Debt costs now are about *half* what they were from 1985 to 1995! Higher debt costs then weren't problematic. Our much lower debt costs now can't possibly be.

Exhibit 13.3   Federal Debt Interest Payments as a Percent of GDP

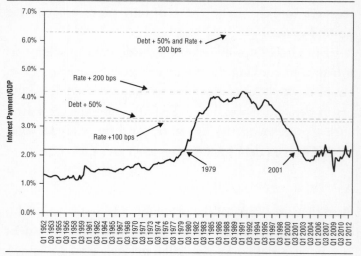

Source: Thomson Reuters, from 12/31/1951 to 06/30/2011.

What's more, either our aggregate debt amount or average interest rate paid or both must move hugely just to get to a level of debt interest payments that still wasn't problematic in the past. First, higher interest payments would affect only newly issued debt, not existing debt. It would take some time for higher rates to materially move impact total interest paid.

Then, too, if average interest rates moved 100 basis points or total net public debt increased 50%, debt costs would still be below levels from 1982 to 1998—again, not alarming. If interest rates jumped 200 basis points, we'd just hit where we were in 1991—at the start of a massive economic boom and bull market. To get to levels never before seen, debt would have to increase 50% *and* interest rates would have to jump 200 basis points. I doubt that happens soon or fast.

Cheaper Debt After the Downgrade

Some may argue increasing debt would make interest rates rise because investors would lose faith. Again, where's the evidence? America's net debt level has been increasing the last few years, yet interest rates have *fallen*.

In fact, America's debt rating was downgraded—and interest rates are lower than before!

For a brief refresher, in August 2011, in the wake of a rancorous debate over raising the US debt ceiling (an arbitrary marker that's been raised over 100 times since it came into existence in 1917 to ease the war-funding effort), S&P downgraded the US from its pristine AAA rating. Folks were fearful that would kick off a crisis of confidence in US debt.

Didn't happen. It was the reverse! US stocks, amid a correction, rallied through year-end 2011 and beyond. As I write in 2012, US stocks are strongly positive for the year.

And a year after the downgrade, across the board, Treasury rates were *lower* than they were. This is exactly opposite of what you'd think would happen if the world believed the US a worse credit risk.

But that's just it. The world *doesn't* think the US is a worse credit risk. That's what the market is telling us. And in fact, S&P doesn't necessarily think it is, either! Its downgrade was based not on fiscal or economic factors, primarily, but on politics. In S&P's opinion, America's two major political parties were unlikely to agree on major budget items. (Why it was news to S&P that politicians can't agree is utterly mystifying to me. But never mind.)

But if you checked history, this shouldn't surprise you. There have been 12 instances when nations have been downgraded from an AAA status (S&P's highest credit rating): Belgium, Ireland, Finland, Italy, Portugal and Spain in 1998; Japan in 2001; Spain and Ireland again in 2009; the US in 2011; and France and Austria in 2012. Exhibit 13.4 shows what happened to benchmark 10-year rates on average in the lead-up to and immediate aftermath of the rating cut.

It's common to see yields spike just a bit right before the rating cut as markets price in fears of the coming cut. But the average spike is 11 basis points—not a huge move. And after the cut? On average, rates fall.

Exhibit 13.4   Debt Rates and S&P Downgrades (10-Year Yields)

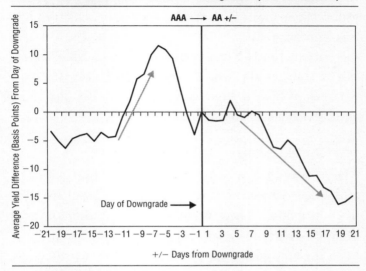

Source: Thomson Reuters, as of 10/25/2012.[1]

Why do markets tend to shrug off credit downgrades to AAA nations? The big three credit ratings agencies (S&P, Moody's and Fitch) are effectively a government-backed oligopoly. Hence, as of now, the raters needn't compete on price or quality. The market usually knows their opinions aren't worth much.

What's more, the raters have a knack for telling us what we already know. And if you base an opinion on the behavior of politicians—politicians who may not be around after the next election—the market has even less reason to care.

Fact is, the US may not be AAA in S&P's eyes, but it still has the world's biggest and deepest credit markets. Which is why America's debt costs are manageable and likely to be for some time.

Dependent on the Kindness of Strangers?

Maybe you buy into that notion—that our ability to afford our debt matters as much as (or more than) relative debt loads. But what about the common fear America is beholden to foreigners?

The story goes: Foreign countries prop up our profligate ways, and we're dangerously beholden to them. Worse, China owns nearly all our debt! (Why China bugs people so much is beyond me. But whenever you read about foreign debt ownership, people make a big deal about China's Treasury holdings. If the Chinese want to lend us money cheaply, I say let 'em.)

Is it true we're dangerously beholden to foreigners? Exhibit 13.5 shows major holders of US debt, and Exhibit 13.6 breaks down the "other" category.

The largest chunk of our debt—36.2%—is held by domestic investors. Individuals, corporations, charities, banks, mutual funds and myriad other entities.

Exhibit 13.5   Who Actually Holds US Government Debt?

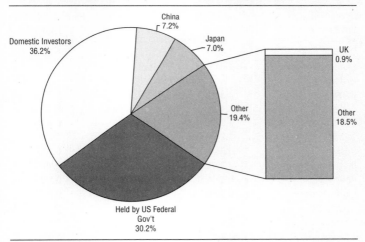

Source: Thomson Reuters, US Department of the Treasury as of 07/31/2012.

The US federal government itself owns 30.2% via intra-governmental agencies. Just 33.6% is held by foreign investors.

And it's not all China. China holds a good chunk—7.2%. Hardly surprising since China is now the world's second largest economy at about 11% of global GDP.[2] Japan holds a near-identical amount—7.0%. But no one much complains about that. (Japan and China often flip-flop as America's largest single foreign creditor.) In the 1980s, folks got kerfuffled over Japan's economic

Exhibit 13.6   "Other" US Lenders

Lender	Percent US Debt Owned	Lender	Percent US Debt Owned
Oil Exporters*	1.65%	Canada	0.36%
Caribbean Banking Centers**	1.61%	Mexico	0.36%
Brazil	1.59%	India	0.33%
All Other	1.42%	Korea, South	0.27%
Switzerland	1.27%	Philippines	0.23%
Taiwan	1.24%	Turkey	0.22%
Russia	0.96%	Poland	0.19%
Belgium	0.89%	Chile	0.19%
Hong Kong	0.88%	Colombia	0.18%
Luxembourg	0.82%	Sweden	0.18%
Ireland	0.58%	Italy	0.17%
Singapore	0.58%	Australia	0.17%
Norway	0.46%	Israel	0.17%
France	0.43%	Netherlands	0.16%
Germany	0.40%	Spain	0.16%
Thailand	0.37%	Malaysia	0.12%

*Ecuador, Venezuela, Indonesia, Bahrain, Iran, Iraq, Kuwait, Oman, Qatar, Saudi Arabia, the United Arab Emirates, Algeria, Gabon, Libya and Nigeria
**Bahamas, Bermuda, British Virgin Islands, Cayman Islands, Netherlands Antilles and Panama.
Source: Thomson Reuters, US Department of the Treasury, as of 07/31/2012.

growth and its purchase of US assets. But then Japan entered a long period of stagnancy—mostly because it doesn't do capitalism right.

Folks who fear China's overtaking the US in economic dominance should know China's growth isn't the organic growth of a free-market democracy.

China's communist government relies on fast growth to keep its urban citizens happy. It uses every lever available to create fast growth in the hopes educated citizens won't notice (or will mind less) their rights' being trampled. (This is a country where a billion people still live in subsistence poverty and a relatively few live in a style we'd call anything like "middle class" in the US.)

China may grow—a lot! Its output may even surpass the US at some point. But China needs more than rising output to challenge the US. Simply, China can't surpass the US in economic dominance until it becomes a true, free-market democracy— which would be a great thing for China, the US and the world.

So Chinese and foreign investors in general don't own scary-sized chunks of our debt. But folks tend to have two additional fears: that foreign holders will sell our debt, and that we won't be able to repay them. And/ or, they'll stop buying our debt, and we won't be able to fund our profligacy anymore. (*If* you believe we're profligate. I don't. I think the government is a stupid spender of your money, but I don't worry about profligacy tied to the earlier point in this chapter about America's debt being affordable.)

Run down this logic train: Why would it be scary if China (or anyone) sold huge chunks of our debt? That debt is a contract. If they want to sell it, there's not some buy-back provision. We don't have to fork over remaining principal all at once. Instead, China would sell its Treasurys on the secondary market. Someone else would buy the debt, and then we'd pay *them* the same interest rate we were paying China. No net impact on America there. We don't care who's holding the debt—we just care that we can make the interest and principal payments. (We can.)

But why would China want to dump a bunch of Treasurys at once? It would increase debt supply on the secondary market. Supply goes up, prices fall. China likely loses money on that trade, which is shooting itself in the foot.

But hang on—bond yields and prices have an inverse relationship. If China floods the market making prices fall, that makes interest rates rise—which makes our super-safe debt that much more enticing at the next auction to someone else! That increases demand, which would push prices up and yields back down. We don't suffer much (if at all) in this scenario—which is unlikely because, again, like the butcher, baker and candlestick maker, China will act in its own best interest. And it isn't in its best interest to dump a bunch of its US debt holdings all at once.

China isn't buying US debt out of charity or some sense of global karma. It doesn't feel obligated to the US. It buys our debt because it satisfies a particular need. In this case, China buys a lot of US debt to manage its currency, and because there aren't any other debt markets that can accomodate China's massive currency reserves.

Nowhere to Go

Then, too, if nations decide not to buy any US debt ... whose debt will they buy? What other options have debt markets as deep? Exhibit 13.7 shows America's net public debt relative to the remaining AAA nations—the likely substitutes for American debt. America's debt is 57.5% of this group. Yes, China and the rest could buy Australia's debt or Canada's or Germany's. And they already do! But they'd have to spread out their debt holdings considerably. Germany is the next largest low-risk issuer of government debt, but its public debt market is just 25% of America's. There's not a terrific full replacement for American debt, and it exposes investors to increased debt rate volatility.

Exhibit 13.7   US and Other Sovereign Debt Issuers

Country	Public Debt ($M)	Public Debt as a % of Total
Australia	$248,222	1.4%
Canada	$1,235,836	6.9%
Denmark	$92,466	0.5%
Finland	$96,325	0.5%
Germany	$2,567,702	14.3%
Hong Kong	$107,036	0.6%
Luxembourg	$7,056	0.0%
Netherlands	$464,941	2.6%
Norway	$154,848	0.9%
Singapore	$376,940	2.1%
Sweden	$144,975	0.8%
Switzerland	$180,361	1.0%
United Kingdom	$1,976,270	11.0%
United States (AA1)	**$10,351,330**	**57.5%**
Total	**$18,004,307**	

Sources: CIA World Factbook 2011, World Bank Quarterly External Debt Statistics, all S&P AAA-rated debt issuers as of 12/31/2011 and the US.

America's debt situation isn't tenuous. We aren't Greece. Not even close! And debt isn't the inherent boogeyman so many believe. Debt, used wisely, is a right and normal part of a healthy economy. Avoiding all debt wouldn't improve anything. There was a point in time when America had no debt—after Andrew Jackson paid off all of America's debt in 1835 with proceeds from Western land sales. Which effectively led to the Panic of 1837 and the Depression of 1837 to 1843—one of the three worst recessions in America's history (the other two started in 1873 and 1929).

Don't fret the aggregate amount of debt. Focus on how affordable it is. And for America, debt is incredibly affordable and likely to remain so for some time.

Chapter Fourteen

Strong Dollar, Strong Stocks

~

"A strong dollar is just better."

THE RELATIVE STRENGTH (or lack thereof) of the US dollar is often cited as a symptom of myriad ills. As in, our economy is weak, therefore the dollar is weak. Our big budget deficit makes foreigners look down at us, weakening the dollar.

And then there's the fear a weak US dollar self-perpetuates further weakness. For example, a weak dollar makes US imports more expensive—and because America is a net importer, that can drag on growth! And many fear a weak dollar portends weak stock returns.

Weak Dollar, Strong Dollar—Does It Matter?

It's true a weak dollar makes imports more expensive. Don't take that to mean a strong dollar is good! Or that when we have a strong dollar, people are happy about it. A strong dollar, as we had periodically in the 1990s, is also often blamed as the root of ills. Folks complain a strong dollar makes our *exports* too expensive, so no one wants to buy them, and that's *also* hard on our economy. It's as if folks believe there's some perfect state of dollar/non-dollar balance—and if we're not at that point, we're headed for ruin.

This is a nonsense myth for several reasons. First, currencies are simply different flavors of money. One isn't inherently better than another. There are both pros and cons to a weak and strong currency. Also, currencies aren't appreciating assets like stocks. They're commodities. If one is weak, it's only weak relative to something else. So the dollar is weak because the euro or pound sterling or a bunch of currencies is strong and vice versa.

See it this way: If you believe a weak dollar is economically bad for the US, then a strong non-dollar must be good for the non-US world. Because the US is just 22% of world GDP,[1] a weak dollar should be, by this theory, *less* bad for the world overall than a strong non-dollar is good! So on balance, a weak dollar should be good. No ... great!

You know in your bones that's silly. But that's the logical conclusion if you believe a weak currency is economically bad—folks just don't often think things through.

Think Inside the 4-Box

The potentially more costly myth is a weak dollar portends weak stock returns. Also nonsense. Weak or strong, the dollar's relative strength doesn't dictate market direction. Use the same logic from before. If the dollar is weak, that means the non-dollar is strong. And if a weak dollar is bad for US stocks, that means the strong non-dollar should be good for non-US stocks. If that were true, we could see it easily in history—US and non-US stocks would flip-flop directionally and be at least modestly negatively correlated.

But the reverse is true. US and non-US stocks usually move in the same direction, as shown in Exhibit 14.1. Not always and not at the same magnitude—but if US stocks are up, non-US stocks tend to be up. When US stocks are down, same thing. Not always

Exhibit 14.1   US Versus Non-US Stocks

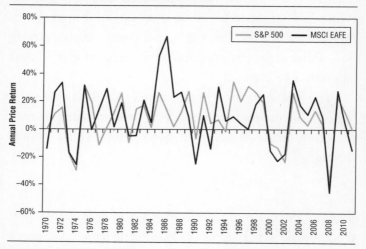

Source: Thomson Reuters, S&P 500 Price Index, MSCI EAFE Price Index, from 12/31/1969 to 12/31/2011.

perfectly, but enough to show US and non-US stocks aren't moving in opposite directions.

Here's another way to test whether dollar direction impacts stocks. I call this a 4-box, and you can use it to test any number of beliefs. Exhibit 14.2 shows the two possible outcomes for US stocks in any given year and their frequencies—up or down. (This shows data back to 1971, which is after the end of the Bretton Woods era when major currencies began truly floating freely.) And it shows the two possible outcomes for the trade-weighted

Exhibit 14.2   US Stocks Versus the US Dollar

		US Stocks		
		Up	Down	Total
US Dollar	Up	17 (41%)	4 (10%)	21 (51%)
	Down	15 (37%)	5 (12%)	20 (49%)
	Total	32 (78%)	9 (22%)	

Source: Global Financial Data, Inc., as of 03/07/2012. Trade-Weighted US Dollar Index,[2] S&P 500 Total Return Index,[3] from 12/31/1970 to 12/31/2011.

dollar and their frequencies. (The trade-weighted dollar is the correct way to do this because what we care about most is how the dollar fares against US trading partners. We don't trade much with Bhutan, so we don't care if the ngultrum is super strong or weak against the dollar.)

Combined, you get frequencies for the four possible annual outcomes: stocks and the dollar both up, stocks up and the dollar down, stocks down and the dollar up, or both down.

First, what should always smack you in the face is US stocks are up more than down—much more—a big 78% in this period. (Get that imprinted in your DNA, and you'll see more investing success: Stocks rise much more than they fall.) Second, whether the dollar was up or down was effectively a coin flip. There's no evidence the dollar is unidirectional.

Then, the most common outcome? The dollar and stocks both up—41% of all years. Which isn't surprising once you accept stocks rise more than fall.

And where's the proof a weak dollar is bad for stocks? If you believe that, the data should show that when the US dollar is down, most often, US stocks are down, too. Not so. When the US dollar was down historically, stocks were three times more likely to be up than down—37% of all years to 12% of all years. (Again, stocks rise more than fall.)

When stocks are down, it's a coin flip whether the dollar is up or down because, in general, it's just a coin flip whether the dollar is up or down. There's no conclusion to be had here regarding the dollar's impact on stock market direction because over long periods, *there is no dollar impact* on stock market direction.

Exhibit 14.3 shows the same thing but with world stocks. Again, world stocks are up more than down. And when the US dollar is down, world stocks are near *four times* as likely to be up versus down (39% of all years versus 10%). And, once more, there's no conclusion to be drawn because dollar direction doesn't impact world stock market direction. Can't get more clear and simple than that.

Now, in the very near term, currency movements can impact your portfolio return. For example, if you're

Strong Dollar, Strong Stocks

Exhibit 14.3   World Stocks Versus the US Dollar

		World Stocks		Total
		Up	Down	
US Dollar	**Up**	15 (37%)	6 (15%)	21 (51%)
	Down	16 (39%)	4 (10%)	20 (49%)
	Total	31 (76%)	10 (22%)	

Source: Global Financial Data, Inc., as of 03/07/2012. Trade-Weighted US Dollar Index,[4] MSCI World Total Return Index with net dividends,[5] from 12/31/1970 to 12/31/2011.

a US investor and own a UK stock, and the stock price doesn't move but pound sterling appreciates 10% versus the dollar, the value of that UK stock has effectively appreciated 10% for you! And if pound sterling falls 10%, then the value of the stock similarly falls for US investors. If currency exchange rates move more than stock prices (as can happen), currency values can have a bigger impact on US dollar returns of foreign stocks than stock prices! Yowza!

If you're a global investor (which I recommend for most stock investors) and are fully and appropriately diversified globally, that's a lot of currencies to track. Should you quit your job now to become a currency trading expert?

Nah. If you have a long time horizon (as most readers of this book likely do), over time, because currencies are inherently zero-sum and irregularly cyclical, currency impacts on a global portfolio net out to close to zero.

What about investing directly in currencies? Feel free, but know currencies are notoriously volatile. Yet, long term, investors don't get paid for that volatility. If you want to trade currencies for gain, you must be a consummate short-term market timer. That's incredibly tough. If you know how to do that well and consistently, then you don't really need my help or this book.

When folks say a too-weak (or sometimes, too-strong) dollar spells doom for stocks, ignore it. There's no evidence it's so, and no fundamental reason for it, either. Alternatively, you could exploit the fear as a minor bullish factor because fear of a false future factor is nearly always bullish. Yes, something might spell doom for stocks, but it won't be the dollar on its own.

Chapter Fifteen

Turmoil Troubles Stocks

~

"Stocks can't rise when the world is so scary."

OFTEN, MEDIA AND PUNDITS tell us things are just "too scary," the news too bad, the world too dangerous for stocks to rise. (More on how to better interpret media in Chapter 16.) Yet the world has always faced risks. Investors may say, "Yes, but that was then, and I always knew those past scary times would work out ok. But *this time it's different.*"

First, as discussed elsewhere in this book, folks always think this time it's different. But it's never so very different as folks fear. This is why Sir John Templeton famously said, "The four most expensive words in the English language are, 'This time, it's different.'"

Among the jumble of evolutionary responses that helped humanity long ago but making investing tougher now: Humans evolved to forget past pain, fast. It was a survival instinct! We may think we were cool as cucumbers when faced with past fears, but the reality is, we very often weren't.

Think we've had a rough few years recently? A major Japanese earthquake and tsunami and nuclear accident. Heightened Middle East tensions. Contentious politics. But are politics *truly* more contentious now? Political rhetoric has always been heated—anyone who tells you we're more divided *now* doesn't know a shred of US history. Political infighting is a constant. (And if you think US politics are heated, you should watch a UK parliamentary session. Heck, in 2012, a male Greek politician punched a female political rival *in the face on live TV*.)

Tensions have been flaring in the Middle East not just since Israel became a nation, but for all its history. (In 1801, the US Marines were dispatched to what's now Libya to protect shipping lines from terrorists—the

Barbary pirates.) And the world has been plagued by natural disasters since, well, the Big Bang. There's no evidence natural disasters are increasing in frequency or ferociousness.

Some folks like to claim even the *weather* is getting more severe and unpredictable for whatever reason, making hurricanes more fierce and such. Which doesn't explain why the 1900 Galveston hurricane was the deadliest to ever make landfall on the US—and the second costliest based on inflation-adjusted dollars. Of the top 10 strongest US land-falling hurricanes, all but 2 were prior to 1970.[1] The most active decade for hurricanes since we've been recording (in 1851) was the 1940s, with 24, followed by the 1880s with 22, and the 1890s and 1910s with 21 each.[2]

Why does that matter? Simply, folks inflate current events in their mind and misremember past events. Think geopolitics are tense now? What about for all of the Cold War? Or during the Cuban Missile Crisis, when missiles were actually aimed at our beds a short boat-ride away from Florida? Think debt is high now? It was well over 100% of GDP in World War II's aftermath. Remember Chernobyl? That accident put Japan's much better contained one in 2011 to shame. In the US, we've seen long periods of food rationing and gas rationing—not just in response to short-lived natural disasters. We've been hit on our own soil in Hawaii, New York and DC and had embassies attacked overseas (not just in 2012, but multiple times before). We've had oil shocks, strikes, recessions, riots, hyperinflation, deflation. Accounting scandals. Impeachments. Homegrown terror attacks on our own soil.

Yet, look at Exhibit 15.1 which shows notable events for each year back to 1934 and annual global stock returns. Through it all, stocks have overall risen. Yes, bear markets occur, but no US or global bear market has ever been predicated by a natural disaster. Outside of the start of World War II in Europe, geopolitical tensions—even outright major terror attacks and the start of hot wars—have had a fleeting, and not necessarily negative, impact on stocks.

History is never pristine. The world can be a pretty darn scary place—there's never a dull moment. Yet, through it all, one constant is the resiliency of capital markets. If you're waiting for things to "calm down" to be invested, you'll be waiting a long time indeed. And if you didn't invest during periods of turmoil, you wouldn't spend much time invested at all—a mistake, since stocks have been up 72% of all years.[3]

How can stocks rise in the face of all this drama and trauma? Scary things are a constant in the world. Ones that are well known get priced into the market quickly. Their presence is just as often good, not bad, for stocks.

Exhibit 15.1   Never a Dull Moment

Year	Events	Stock Returns
1934	Massive Wall Street reforms passed; National Recovery Act price controls; Hitler declares himself Führer	2.55%
1935	Italy invades Africa; Hitler rejects Versailles treaty; Dust Bowl; Social Security Act; NRA overturned	22.78%
1936	Hitler occupies Rhineland; Nazi appeasement; Spanish Civil War; Top US tax bracket hits 79%	19.28%
1937	Short but sharp US recession; Capital spending & industrial production drop; Japan invades China	−16.95%
1938	Nazis annex Austria and invade Czechoslovakia; New England hit by major hurricane	5.61%
1939	Germany & Italy sign military pact; Britain, France and Poland ally; Poland invaded, beginning World War II	−1.44%
1940	France falls to Hitler; Battle of Britain; Top US income tax bracket over 81%; Wall Street regulations passed	3.53%
1941	Pearl Harbor; Germany invades USSR; US declares war on Japan, Italy & Germany	18.74%
1942	Wartime price controls; Battle of Midway; Top US income tax bracket 88%	1.19%
1943	US Meat & Cheese rationed; Price & wage controls; Major U-boat attacks; Fed. deficit exceeds 30% of US GDP	19.89%
1944	Consumer goods shortages; Allies invade Normandy; Top US income tax bracket hits record 94%	−10.24%
1945	Postwar recession predicted; Invasion of Iwo Jima; FDR dies; Atom bomb dropped in Japan	11.03%
1946	US net debt exceeds 100% of GDP; Employment Act of 1946 passed; Steel & shipyard workers strike	−15.12%
1947	Cold War; High US inflation; Israel/Palestine debate swirls; Indo-Pakistani War; Communists take Hungary	3.20%
1948	Berlin blockade; US seizes railroads to avert strike; Israel independence, immediately invaded; US recession	−5.73%
1949	Russia explodes atom bomb; Britain devalues the pound; Communists control China; Taiwan/China tensions	5.42%

(Continued)

Exhibit 15.1 (*Continued*)

Year	Events	Stock Returns
1950	Korean War; McCarthy and the "Red Scare"; China invades Tibet; Global population exceeds 2.5 billion	25.48%
1951	Excess Profits Tax; Rosenberg trial; Korean War continues; US tests H-bomb; Marshall Plan ends	22.45%
1952	US seizes steel mills to avert strike; Egyptian revolution; Jordanian coup; America's polio scare hits a high	15.82%
1953	Europe hit by North Sea floods; Russia explodes H-bomb; Tecession; Stalin dies; Korean War ends	4.84%
1954	Dow 300—fear of heights; Taiwan/China conflict; French-Indochina War; *Brown v. Board* integration debate	49.82%
1955	Eisenhower illness; Warsaw Pact formed; North Vietnam invades South; US 7th Fleet aids Taiwan's army	24.74%
1956	Suez Crisis—Israel and Egypt fight; Asian flu; Hungarian Revolution crushed by Soviets	6.58%
1957	Russia launches Sputnik; Recession; Little Rock Central High integration crisis; Eisenhower suffers stroke	−6.02%
1958	Recession; Taiwan/China conflict; Marines dispatched to Beirut; Khrushchev attempts to unify control of Berlin	34.46%
1959	Castro seizes power in Cuba; US steel strikes; Cuban-backed revolt in Dominican Republic fails	23.30%
1960	Recession; Russia downs U-2 spy plane; Castro nationalizes foreign property; Global population over 3 billion	3.49%
1961	Berlin Wall erected; Green Berets sent to Vietnam; Bay of Pigs invasion fails; Freedom Riders—civil rights	20.78%
1962	Cuban Missile Crisis; JFK cracks down on steel prices, Cuba embargo; China/India fight	−6.21%
1963	President Kennedy assassinated; South Vietnam government overthrown; Integration/segregation debates intensify	15.38%
1964	Gulf of Tonkin; Race riots; Brazil coup d'état; Segregation abolished; Khrushchev deposed	11.25%
1965	Civil rights marches; Regular US troops in Vietnam; India-Pakistan war; Major blackout in Northeast US affecting 30 million	9.83%

Exhibit 15.1 (*Continued*)

Year	Events	Stock Returns
1966	Vietnam War escalates; Nigerian coup; Chinese Cultural Revolution begins	−10.12%
1967	US race riots; British Parliament votes to nationalize 90% of steel industry; Six-Day War	21.28%
1968	USS *Pueblo* seized; Tet Offensive; Martin Luther King & RFK assassinated; Soviets quash Prague Spring	13.94%
1969	US recession; Prime rate at record high; N. Korea downs US navy plane; Ghadafi takes Libya	−3.86%
1970	US invades Cambodia; Bankruptcy of Penn Central; Aussie Poseidon bubble bursts; Kent State shootings	−3.08%
1971	Wage & price freezes; Bretton-Woods era ends, gold standard abolished; US dollar devalued	18.36%
1972	US mines Vietnamese ports; Israeli athletes murdered at Munich Olympics; Iraq nationalizes oil companies	22.48%
1973	Energy crisis—Arab oil embargo; US recession begins; Watergate scandal; Agnew resigns; Yom Kippur War	−15.24%
1974	Steepest market drop in four decades; Nixon resigns; Yen devalued; Franklin National Bank collapses	−25.47%
1975	NYC bankrupt; North Vietnam wins war; UK nationalizes automaker; Spanish dictator Francisco Franco dies	32.80%
1976	OPEC raises oil prices; US government takes over many private railroads; Lebanese Civil War	13.40%
1977	Social Security taxes raised; Spanish neo-fascists attack during political assembly; NYC blackout	0.68%
1978	Rising interest rates; US net debt crosses $600 billion, double 1970s level; Cleveland, Ohio defaults	16.52%
1979	CPI inflation spikes; Three Mile Island nuclear disaster; Iran seizes US embassy; USSR invades Afghanistan	10.95%
1980	All-time-high interest rates; Love Canal; Iran-Iraq War; Chrysler bailout; Silver crash	25.67%
1981	Steep recession begins; Reagan shot; Energy bubble bursts; AIDS identified for first time; Israel bombs Iraqi nuclear facility	−4.79%

(*Continued*)

Exhibit 15.1 (*Continued*)

Year	Events	Stock Returns
1982	Worst recession in 40 years—profits plummet; Unemployment spikes; Falklands War; US embargoes Libyan oil	9.71%
1983	US invades Grenada; US embassy in Beirut bombed; WPPSS biggest muni-bond default ever; US net debt hits $1 trillion	21.93%
1984	Then-record federal deficit; FDIC bails out Continental Illinois; AT&T monopoly broken up; Persian Gulf Tanker Wars; Union Carbide Bhopal leak	4.72%
1985	Arms race; Ohio banks closed to stop run; US is largest debtor nation; Net debt hits $1.5 trillion—double 1980 level	40.56%
1986	US bombs Libya; Boesky pleads guilty to insider trading; *Challenger* explodes; Chernobyl	41.89%
1987	Record-setting single-day market decline; Iran-Contra investigation blames Reagan; World population hits 5 billion	16.16%
1988	First Republic Bank fails; Noriega indicted by US; Pan Am 103 bombing; UK's "Big Bang" financial market reforms	23.29%
1989	Tiananmen Square; SF earthquake; US troops deploy in Panama; *Exxon Valdez* spill; S&L crisis—over 500 banks fail, RTC formed	16.61%
1990	Recession; Consumer confidence plummets; Iraq invades Kuwait—tensions rise; German reunification fears	−17.02%
1991	US begins air war in Iraq; Unemployment rises to 7%; Irish terrorists attack 10 Downing Street; USSR collapses	18.28%
1992	Hurricane Andrew devastates Florida; Riots in LA; Recession fears; Bitter election contest	−5.23%
1993	Tax increase; World Trade Center bombed; European double-dip recession; British pound devalued	22.50%
1994	Attempted nationalized health care; Mexican peso crisis; Former Yugoslavia descends into civil war; Kim Il Sung dies	5.08%
1995	Weak dollar panic; Clinton bails out Mexico; Aum Shinrikyo sarin gas attacks in Japan; Oklahoma City bombing	20.72%

Exhibit 15.1 (*Continued*)

Year	Events	Stock Returns
1996	Fears of inflation; Whitewater investigation; Khobar Towers bombing; Greenspan cites investors' "irrational exuberance"	13.48%
1997	Tech "mini-crash" in October & "Pacific Rim crisis"; China takes control of Hong Kong; Iraq disarmament crisis	15.76%
1998	Russian ruble crisis; "Asian flu"; Long-term Capital Management debacle; US embassy bombings in Africa	24.34%
1999	Y2K paranoia & correction; Clinton impeached; Venezuela's Hugo Chavez takes power; War in Balkans	24.93%
2000	Dot-com bubble begins to burst; *Gore v. Bush*—contested presidential election; USS *Cole* bombed	−13.18%
2001	Recession; September 11 terrorist attacks; IRA bombs BBC; US-Afghan War; Then-contentious Patriot Act becomes law	−16.82%
2002	Corporate accounting scandals; Sarbanes-Oxley Act passed; Terrorism fears; Tensions with Iraq and "Axis of Evil"	−19.89%
2003	Mutual fund scandals; Conflict in Iraq; SARS; Space shuttle *Columbia* explodes; Israeli airstrikes within Syria	33.11%
2004	Fears of a weak dollar and US "triple deficits"; Madrid train bombings; Indian Ocean tsunami kills over 100,000	14.72%
2005	Tension with North Korea & Iran over nuclear arms; Hurricane Katrina; Oil price spikes to $70; 7/7 London bombings	9.49%
2006	North Korea testing nuclear weapons; Continued war in Iraq & Afghanistan; Mexican Drug War begins	20.07%
2007	Financials firms take writedowns; Significant accounting rule change; Israel strikes suspected Syrian nuclear facility; Subprime fears	9.04%
2008	Global financial panic; Steepest calendar-year stock market declines since 1930s; Oil exceeds $140; Government bailouts	−40.71%
2009	Unemployment exceeds 10%; Massive global fiscal and monetary stimulus; US auto bailouts	29.99%

(*Continued*)

Exhibit 15.1 (*Continued*)

Year	Events	Stock Returns
2010	PIIGS sovereign debt scares; Double-dip recession fears; "Flash Crash"; US health-care and financial reform laws passed	11.76%
2011	Arab spring; Japanese earthquake and tsunami; Continuing PIIGS sovereign debt concerns; Bin Laden killed; US downgraded	−5.54%

Sources: Global Financial Data, Inc., as of 08/28/2012; Thomson Reuters. Returns from 1970 to 2011 reflect the Morgan Stanley Capital International (MSCI) World Index, which measures the performance of selected stocks in 24 developed countries and is presented inclusive of dividends and withholding taxes. Returns prior to 1970 are provided by Global Financial Data, Inc., and simulate how a world index, inclusive of dividends, would have performed had it been calculated back to 1934.

Then, too, remember that in the near term, stocks can wildly wiggle. But over time, their upward sweep represents the potentially infinite upward sweep of profits. As mentioned throughout the book, profit motive is an intensely powerful positive force. It's at the root of capitalism and the reason free, democratic, capitalistic nations thrive and less-free nations don't. Profit motive isn't sapped because humanity faces challenges. In fact, challenges and the need for innovation can be motivating factors for those willing to take risks to chase future profits. Capital markets are resilient because humanity is resilient. Those who've bet against that have been proven wrong, time and again.

Chapter Sixteen

News You Can Use

~

"I heard it in the news, so it must be so."

THAT, ALONG WITH "this time it's different," has to be one of the more expensive phrases in the English language.

In the 28 (plus) years (and going) I've written the "Portfolio Strategy" column for *Forbes*, I've often written about the challenges (and opportunities) in interpreting media. In my March 13, 1995, *Forbes* column,

"Advanced Fad Avoidance," one of the tips I included to avoid falling prey to harmful fads was:

> If you read or hear about some investment idea or significant event more than once in the media, it won't work. By the time several commentators have thought and written about it, even new news is too old.

Some will read that and the other things I've written on media and wrongly think I mean news is bad and should be ignored. No! News is your friend as an investor! Don't ignore it. Rather, learn to interpret it differently and more correctly, which overall and on average can give you an investing edge.

Look the Other Way

First, reading news tells you what everyone is focused on. A valuable service performed for you for free!

Most people know to make a successful market bet, they should know something most other folks don't. But they don't know where to begin to know what others don't! An easy way to start is simply knowing what everyone else is focusing on—and *looking away*. You can use the news for that.

The stock market is an efficient discounter of all widely known information. If you can easily find something online, in print, on TV, anywhere in our 24/7 news cycle—where information flies around the world with the click of a button—that news is likely already largely reflected in current stock prices. Or it will be soon and so fast, your chance to trade on it has likely passed. And the longer something appears as a headline story, the more its power to move markets has been sapped.

That doesn't mean if bad news comes out, stocks can't drop. They might! News can impact sentiment, and sentiment moves fast. Trying to time short-term swings can be perilous. You likely end up whipsawed more often than not. And initial sentiment reactions to bad news are often hugely overdone. If you sell on the bad news, you may end up selling low and missing a better time to get out later—*if* the bad news is indeed so very bad. Plus, there's nothing guaranteeing what you buy to replace the stock you sold only rises. Selling on bad news and bad news alone can mean buying high, selling low and potentially missing out on a rebound.

Then, too, whether stocks are falling or rising, often it's some other factor (or, likely, group of factors) than what's widely discussed in media making that move happen.

Which means if everyone is focused on something, you know you can safely ignore that and look the other way. At what folks *aren't* focusing on. At those things that actually may have material future market-moving power. They're looking in the rearview mirror, thinking it can tell them what's ahead. That never works and sometimes leads to disaster.

Look away. If you can do that, you can have an edge over other investors. Heck—over most professionals! But if you're looking at the same news everyone else is and interpreting it the same way, you likely miss what those other factors are. You're moving with the herd.

A Sentiment Indicator

News is also a good sentiment indicator. Sentiment is key because over the next 12 to 24 months or so, it's effectively interchangeable with *demand*. (Revisit Chapter 9 for more on demand.) If you understand where sentiment currently is and can develop a good hypothesis for whether it will rise or fall, you can know pretty well if stocks are likelier to rise or fall.

You will hate my saying this, but measuring sentiment is often as much (or more) art as science. Lots of folks use consumer confidence indexes—the University of Michigan and Conference Board publish two popular ones—to measure sentiment.

Except every sentiment index I've seen is flawed. They're built, usually, to give you a decent snapshot of how people felt on average ... *last* month. To be more exact, the indexes are an averaging of how people felt in the *middle* of the previous month. They're coincident at best, but more backward looking. If stocks are *forward* looking (they are), knowing how people felt on average in the middle of the past month does exactly zero for you. There's no evidence any confidence surveys are reliably predictive.

But if you scan three or four national or global newspapers daily, you can get a good feel for general mindset. Media, consumed correctly, can give you, quickly and easily, a broad-strokes feel for sentiment.

What you're really looking for are sentiment extremes. Extreme euphoria is typically a bad sign— you see it at nearly every bull market top. Similarly, extreme negativity is characteristic of the bottoming period of a bear market. In-between sentiment is quite normal, and sentiment can swing fairly broadly within a bull market over short periods.

Interpret It to Use It

Yes, news can be a good source of information—if you know how to interpret it and use it. For that, you must understand what the media industry is and is not.

Most media outfits are *for-profit* businesses. They don't deliver your paper each day (for those remaining that still do a print edition) in a white car with a red cross on the side. They aren't in it for the sake of humanity—they want to turn a profit. In fact, they *must* turn a profit, or they cease to be. And there's nothing wrong with that! Chasing profits is right and noble. It's what allows firms to add shareholder value, hire, pay salaries, provide benefits, etc. All things people like.

To remain afloat, many major media organizations sell subscriptions, and some very few are even successfully selling online subscriptions. But their bread and butter is now, always has been and always will be selling advertising.

To garner higher advertising revenues, they must get eyeballs. The more eyeballs they can deliver, the more their advertisers are willing to pay them for real estate—whether online or in print.

You've heard the saying, "If it bleeds, it leads." It's true! Because news programmers know, if they lead the evening news with a heart-warming story of a Girl Scout who won a $1,000 scholarship for her civics essay, no one will watch. They know they must lead with fire, mayhem, riots, robbery, murder, intrigue.

This isn't by accident. This is because, as discussed in Chapter 1, human beings evolved to be hypersensitive to danger (to better avoid attack by beasts, starvation, freezing to death, etc.)

Which means, because of ingrained evolutionary responses, investors will often take action to avoid the possibility of near-term loss—even if it means harming themselves more in the long run and robbing themselves of superior returns (once again, that concept of *myopic loss aversion*).

Which is why bad news sells. Just a fact. You know that instinctively. When news outfits cover negative news, that's a business decision, pure and simple, to gain eyeballs. There's nothing wrong with that! If you like reading a newspaper, you want it to be profitable. And being profitable means the media will often lead with what humanity naturally will be most interested in.

Said differently: Highlighting positives can sap profits. So if you think, "All I hear or read is bad news!" that's probably true! But it's not necessarily because all is bad in the world. Rather, that's just media firms trying to maximize profits.

Ground Rules for Interpreting Media Profitably

Knowing how the media operates and why, how can you be a better news consumer and actually glean something useful? By following a few ground rules.

1. Media reports *news*—by definition, this is what has already happened. But stocks are forward looking!

   If the media is reporting something, the time to react and trade on that particular news item has likely passed.

2. Stocks reflect all widely known information.

   That doesn't mean, in the near term, the stock market is always correct. It isn't! Because people aren't always correct. Rather, the stock market reflects widely held views.

3. As such, forecasting market direction is about measuring relative expectations.

   When forecasting stocks over the next 12 to 24 months, reality can matter less than what is expected to happen. Understand what most people expect and craft reasonable probabilities around what you think is likely to happen. It's that gap between reality and expectations that will drive stocks.

4. Don't be a contrarian.

   It can be tempting but won't help you any more than following the crowd. Just because the media says something is so, it doesn't mean the opposite is true. It just might mean the expected impact is under- or overstated. *Just because they say something is so doesn't mean it is.* Make that a mantra.

5. Always put data in proper context and ignore the author's point of view.

Journalists know giving the straight *who/what/where/when/why/how* may not always get eyeballs. They may include an exciting narrative that increases entertainment factor, but might obscure reality. Or they may use anecdotes, which are compelling but may not be statistically significant. That's fine! Most people won't read the paper if it's a snooze-fest. But that can be less useful if you are trying to measure likely market impact. Mentally put a line through adjectives and adverbs, ignore anecdotes unless they highlight something fundamental and isolate the facts. Then consider them in context. Scale the number. Ask, "What's the global impact?"

6. Be politically agnostic.

Many people have an ideology they view as correct. And that's ok! But ideology is another form of bias that can blind you.

A subset of this is you should avoid thinking, "Well, I typically agree with this set of people, which means they're always infallibly right." Vary what you read, and be an equal-opportunity skeptic.

Follow those ground rules and you'll be a better, more informed consumer of media. Don't ignore media—use it to your advantage.

Chapter Seventeen

Too Good to Be True

~

*"You've got to get in on this!
This investment seems
too good to be true!"*

WARNING: Too good to be true nearly always is.

In my 2009 book, *How to Smell a Rat*, I wrote about the five signs of financial fraud. This was in the wake of the massive, billion-dollar, decades-long Madoff Ponzi fraud's coming to light—made more tragic because it was easily avoidable. How so? The key decision maker was also the custodian—the number-one sign a Ponzi is possible.

What does that mean? Madoff was responsible for deciding what to buy and sell and when for client portfolios. And clients deposited funds with Madoff Investment Securities. The fox was guarding the hen house.

Madoff founded Madoff Securities in 1960, and it was then and appears now to have always been a legit brokerage—it had been one of America's biggest market-makers in both NYSE and NASDAQ securities. The brokerage firm wasn't the problem—not on its own. The problem was Madoff controlled it *and* the hedge fund. Because Madoff controlled both the advisory and the custody sides, it was technically nothing for him to dummy up statements and take money out the backdoor—for years!

This is the basic structure for every financial Ponzi I've studied. Either the adviser and the custodian were ultimately under singular control, or the adviser had some form of influence over the custodian. And amazingly, in the tsunami of reporting that followed the Madoff and Stanford Ponzi scandals, none I saw focused on this key factor.

Separate Decision Maker and Custody

If you separate the two—insist your funds be held in a separate, well-known national custodian, where you deposit money yourself in an account in your own name (or yours and your spouse's, or in your trust's name, etc.)—you make a financial Ponzi scheme near-impossible.

Still, not *every* outfit that's both adviser and custodian is sure to defraud you. I personally set my business up with the two functions separated to protect my clients from employees going rogue. Or from me going rogue! (There are some reports that Madoff didn't start out intending to defraud. But he started faking account statements after normal market downside resulted in poor returns. Someone with such a fragile ego has no business managing money for other people.) But there are legitimate reasons an adviser may decide to also custody—an additional reason to be aware of the other four signs of potential financial fraud.

1. *Your adviser also has custody of your assets.*
2. Returns are consistently great! Almost *too good to be true.*
3. The investing strategy isn't understandable, is murky, flashy, or "too complicated" for him (her or it) to describe so you easily understand.
4. Your adviser promotes benefits, like exclusivity, which don't impact results.
5. You didn't do your own due diligence, but a trusted intermediary did.

You should do due diligence on any firm you hire. But a firm with one sign merits a deeper look. Be exceedingly wary if there are multiple. Better to be suspicious and safe than trusting and sorry.

And the idea that returns "too good to be true" may be valid can be particularly damaging.

High and Steady ... and Fake

There are two basic camps here—either should make you skeptical. The first are eerily steady returns. This was Madoff's game. Each and every year, he reported client returns of about 10% to 12%. Market up big? His returns were 10% to 12%. Market down big? Returns were still about 10% to 12%. Even month-to-month returns were steady.[1] No big down months or years. A dream come true that was actually a nightmare—usually the case with too-good-to-be-true returns.

That steadiness is like a narcotic. It appeals to our caveman brains and makes us not question too hard— con artists hate getting questioned hard. But such steadiness should immediately be a red flag.

Why would 10% annual returns be alarming? After all, stocks have returned an annualized 10% over long periods.[2] But that's an *average* and, obviously, bakes in huge variability. Years when annual stock returns are around 10% are actually quite rare. Much more often they're up big or down, as shown in Exhibit 7.1 in Chapter 7. Knowing this—accepting in their bones that stocks' returns are naturally variable would have been an additional layer of protection for Madoff's would-be victims—and many other victims of countless Ponzis over the years. Returns so steady aren't just a deviation from reality—they're an outright sign something may be drastically awry.

Now, that probably wouldn't be true if the returns were *low* and steady. Sure, portfolios with lower shorter-term volatility (i.e., a much smaller share of equities) can certainly feature less-variable annual returns. But that would mean returns wouldn't be anything close to equities' long-term average. And even a portfolio with heavy allocations of fixed income would have down years. It would require a portfolio heavily allocated to cash or near-cash instruments to have no negative annual returns—*before* you account for inflation.

A portfolio with long-term returns about matching equities' long-term average should, on average, feature equity-like volatility. No way around it. Be exceedingly suspicious if someone sells you a portfolio with long-term equity-like returns with minimal volatility. Better yet, be out the door.

Super-High ... and Also Fake

The second common Ponzi con tactic is promising huge, mega-outsized returns. The former tactic appeals to our natural dislike of volatility. The latter is about greed—pure and simple.

This was convicted-fraudster Sir Stanford's game. His Antiguan-based bank sold $8 billion in CDs with impossibly high rates—at times topping 16%! Actual CDs from real banks were offering rates as much as half that.[3] But other scamsters historically have done the same thing—guaranteeing huge, way-above-equity-like returns or otherwise unreasonably high returns given the underlying asset, often for very short-term investments. Double your money in three months! That sort of thing.

The red flags are many. Primarily, no one can legally guarantee you anything. Yes, Treasurys are guaranteed inasmuch as the principal and interest payments are backed by the full faith and credit of the US government. If you buy a Treasury and hold to maturity, the US government promises you'll get your principal back with interest paid on time. But if you sell before maturity, you can lose money. (See Chapter 1.) Any investment guarantee from anyone other than the US government *should be considered a scam*.

Even annuities, which can come with guarantees because they're insurance contracts, still feature a warning the annuity is only as good as the insurance firm is solvent. (For more on annuities and why they're usually not a good alternative for investors seeking long-term growth, see Chapters 15 and 16 in my 2009 book, *Debunkery*.)

Too-good-to-be-true scams don't just involve standard investment vehicles like stocks, bonds, CDs, etc. I can't guarantee you anything because, again, no one can or should. But I can *near*-guarantee if someone approaches you with a can't-lose investment with super-high guaranteed returns, it's very likely a scam.

Scams of All Stripes

By now, hopefully, most readers are familiar with the "Nigerian" scam (also known as a 419 fraud—from the section of the Nigerian criminal code)—usually obvious, poorly worded appeals via email from someone claiming to be disgraced royalty who needs your help getting $25 million out of some war-torn nation. There are many derivatives, but know this: If someone asks you to forward them money to help them liberate a bigger chunk of money that they'll share with you, it's a scam.

Other scams aren't so obvious—aside from the guarantee they can't legally make for unrealistic returns. Like the Iraqi dinar scam. In this, victims are approached via email or Internet ads to buy Iraqi dinars. Huge returns are promised from the strengthening dinar. And there are legitimate exchanges if you have legitimate business in Iraqi. But most Internet dinar exchange solicitations are outright scams. And anyone promising you huge returns for arbitraging *any* currency exchange rates is probably a con artist.

Another popular scam in recent years is the ATM leaseback scam. Here, con artists offer to buy ATM machines on your behalf, and you lease them back to them. They manage them for you and promise you a guaranteed monthly stream of income. You can legitimately buy ATMs and manage them if you want. That's not what this is, though. You know it's a scam because they tell you they need $12,000 or more up front to buy the machine—real ones run much less, maybe between $2,000 to $5,000. And they also guarantee you a monthly profit, which, of course, they cannot do. You can go to the FBI's fraud section to review current popular frauds to better arm yourself against con artists (www.fbi.gov/scams-safety/fraud).

No matter the scam, the con artist may lull marks into believing it's legit by sending them monthly or

quarterly checks—at first. Rarely a return on investment, this is more likely cash flow from newer incoming
marks—classic pyramid style. They may try to keep initial victims happy because they can use them to help sell
the con to future marks. Con artists often use victims to
appeal to that victim's social circle. Your friends, col-
leagues and/or church group may not know the con artist from Adam, but they know you! And trust you. And
if you got a couple of checks and are happy, that's a big
vote of confidence in the fraudster. The fraudster may
exploit that confidence to net more of your friends as
victims. It's a dirty game.

The moral of the story? If it seems too good to be
true, it probably is. That's no myth.

Notes

Chapter One: Bonds Are Safer Than Stocks

1. The S&P 500 Total Return Index is based upon GFD calculations of total returns before 1971. These are estimates by GFD to calculate the values of the S&P Composite before 1971 and are not official values. GFD used data from the Cowles Commission and from S&P itself to calculate total returns for the S&P Composite using the S&P Composite Price Index and dividend yields through 1970, official monthly numbers from 1971 to 1987 and official daily data from 1988 on.
2. Ibid.
3. See note 1.
4. See note 1.
5. Global Financial Data, Inc., as of 07/10/2012, S&P 500 Total Return Index, 10-Year US Government Bond Total Return Index from 12/31/1925 to 12/31/2011; see note 1.

6. Ibid.
7. Ibid.
8. Jeremy Warner, "High Energy Prices Need Not Mean Doom," *Sydney Morning Herald*, January 21, 2011.
9. International Monetary Fund, World Economic Outlook Database, October 2012, from 1980 through 2012 (estimate), chained 2005 dollars.

Chapter Two: Asset Allocation Short-Cuts

1. Gary P. Brinson, L. Randolph Hood and Gilbert L. Beebower, "Determinants of Portfolio Performance," *Financial Analysts Journal*, July/August 1986.
2. Global Financial Data, Inc., as of 05/22/2012, annualized average of Consumer Price Index from 12/31/1925 to 12/31/2011.

Chapter Four: More Volatile Than Ever

1. Global Financial Data, Inc., as of 9/20/12, S&P 500 Total Return Index from 12/31/2007 to 12/31/2008 and from 12/31/2008 to 12/31/2009.
2. Global Financial Data, Inc., as of 9/20/12, S&P 500 Total Return Index from 12/31/1925 to 12/31/2011. The S&P 500 Total Return Index is based upon GFD calculations of total returns before 1971. These are estimates by GFD to calculate the values of the S&P Composite before 1971 and are not official values. GFD used data from the Cowles Commission and from S&P itself to calculate total returns for the S&P Composite using the S&P Composite Price Index and dividend yields through 1970, official monthly numbers from 1971 to 1987 and official daily data from 1988 on.

3. The S&P 500 Total Return Index is based upon GFD calculations of total returns before 1971. These are estimates by GFD to calculate the values of the S&P Composite before 1971 and are not official values. GFD used data from the Cowles Commission and from S&P itself to calculate total returns for the S&P Composite using the S&P Composite Price Index and dividend yields through 1970, official monthly numbers from 1971 to 1987 and official daily data from 1988 on.

4. Global Financial Data, Inc., as of 09/20/12, S&P 500 Total Return Index from 12/31/1931 to 12/31/1932; see note 3.

5. Global Financial Data, Inc., as of 09/20/12, S&P 500 Total Return Index from 12/31/1932 to 12/31/1933; see note 3.

6. Global Financial Data, Inc., as of 09/20/12, S&P 500 Total Return Index from 12/31/1997 to 12/31/1998.

7. Global Financial Data, Inc., as of 09/20/12, S&P 500 Total Return Index from 12/31/2009 to 12/31/2010.

8. Global Financial Data, Inc., as of 09/20/12, S&P 500 Total Return Index from 12/31/1979 to 12/31/1980; see note 3.

9. Global Financial Data, Inc., as of 09/20/12, S&P 500 Total Return Index from 12/31/1976 to 12/31/1977; see note 3.

10. Global Financial Data, Inc., as of 09/20/12, S&P 500 Total Return Index from 12/31/1952 to 12/31/1953; see note 3.

11. Global Financial Data, Inc., as of 09/20/12, S&P 500 Total Return Index from 12/31/2004 to 12/31/2005.

12. Global Financial Data, Inc., as of 09/20/12, S&P 500 Total Return Index from 12/31/1950 to 12/31/1951; see note 3.

13. Global Financial Data, Inc., as of 09/20/12, S&P 500 Total Return Index from 12/31/1972 to 12/31/1973; see note 3.

Chapter Five: The Holy Grail—Capital Preservation and Growth

1. Global Financial Data, Inc., as of 05/22/2012, annualized average of Consumer Price Index from 12/31/1925 to 12/31/2011.

2. Bloomberg Finance, L.P., as of 10/25/2012.

3. Ibid.

Chapter Six: The GDP–Stock Mismatch Crash

1. Global Financial Data, Inc., as of 07/10/2012, S&P 500 Total Return Index annualized returns from 12/31/1925 to 12/31/2011 is 9.7%. The S&P 500 Total Return Index is based upon GFD calculations of total returns before 1971. These are estimates by GFD to calculate the values of the S&P Composite before 1971 and are not official values. GFD used data from the Cowles Commission and from S&P itself to calculate total returns for the S&P Composite using the S&P Composite Price Index and dividend yields through 1970, official monthly numbers from 1971 to 1987 and official daily data from 1988.

2. US Bureau of Economic Analysis, as of 12/31/2011.

3. The S&P 500 Total Return Index is based upon GFD calculations of total returns before 1971. These are estimates by GFD to calculate the values of the S&P Composite before 1971 and are not official values. GFD used data from the Cowles Commission and from S&P itself to calculate total returns for the S&P Composite using the S&P Composite Price Index and dividend yields through 1970, official monthly numbers from 1971 to 1987 and official daily data from 1988.

4. Ibid.

Chapter Seven: 10% Forever!

1. The S&P 500 Total Return Index is based upon GFD calculations of total returns before 1971. These are estimates by GFD to calculate the values of the S&P Composite before 1971 and are not official values. GFD used data from the Cowles Commission and from S&P itself to calculate total returns for the S&P Composite using the S&P Composite Price Index and dividend yields through 1970, official monthly numbers from 1971 to 1987 and official daily data from 1988 on.

2. Bankrate.com, as of 11/12/2012.

3. Bloomberg Finance, L.P., as of 10/25/2012; Global Financial Data, Inc., as of 05/22/2012; Consumer Price Index return from 12/31/1925 to 12/31/2011.

4. Bank of America Merrill Lynch US Corporate AAA 7-10 Year Index as of 09/12/2012.

5. Bank of America Merrill Lynch US Corporate High-Yield 7-10 Year Index as of 09/1/2012.

Chapter Nine: The Perma-Superiority of Small-Cap Value

1. Ibbotsen, Ibbotsen US Small Stock Total Return, S&P 500 Total Return from 02/01/1926 to 09/30/2012.

2. Russell 2000, Russell 2000 Value, Russell 2000 Growth, MSCI EAFE; Barclays Aggregate, S&P/Citigroup Primary Growth, S&P/Citigroup Primary Value, S&P 500 Value from 12/31/1990 to 12/31/2010. All returns total returns except MSCI EAFE, which is net. S&P/Citigroup Primary Value index measures the performance of the value style of investing in large-cap US stocks. The index is constructed by dividing the top 80% of all US stocks in terms of market capitalization into a Value index, using style. S&P/Citigroup Primary Growth index measures the performance of the growth style of investing in large-cap US stocks. The index is constructed by dividing the top 80% of all US stocks in terms of market capitalization into a Growth index, using style.

Chapter Ten: Wait Until You're Sure

1. The S&P 500 Total Return Index is based upon GFD calculations of total returns before 1971. These are estimates by GFD to calculate the values of the S&P Composite before 1971 and are not official values. GFD used data from the Cowles Commission and from S&P itself to calculate total returns for the S&P Composite using the S&P Composite Price Index and dividend yields through 1970, official monthly numbers from 1971 to 1987 and official daily data from 1988 on.

2. Ibid.
3. Ibid.
4. Ibid.
5. Global Financial Data, Inc., as of 10/25/2012, S&P 500 price returns.

Chapter Twelve: High Unemployment Kills Stocks

1. The S&P 500 Total Return Index is based upon GFD calculations of total returns before 1971. These are estimates by GFD to calculate the values of the S&P Composite before 1971 and are not official values. GFD used data from the Cowles Commission and from S&P itself to calculate total returns for the S&P Composite using the S&P Composite Price Index and dividend yields through 1970, official monthly numbers from 1971 to 1987 and official daily data from 1988 on.
2. Thomson Reuters, US Bureau of Economic Analysis, as of 05/15/2012.
3. Thomson Reuters, Personal Consumption Expenditures as of 08/31/2012.

Chapter Thirteen: Overindebted America

1. The following nations were downgraded from AAA on these dates: Belgium, Ireland, Finland, Italy, Portugal, Spain on 05/06/1998; Japan on 02/22/2001; Spain on 01/19/2009; Ireland on 03/30/2009; the US on 08/05/2011; France and Austria on 01/13/2012.
2. International Monetary Fund, World Economic Outlook Database, April 2012.

Chapter Fourteen: Strong Dollar, Strong Stocks

1. International Monetary Fund Economic Outlook Database, April 2012.

2. The trade-weighted United States dollar index is computed by the Federal Reserve. The base is 1975–76 = 100 and 10 countries are used in computing the index. The index includes the G-10 countries (Belgium, Canada, France, Germany, Italy, Japan, Netherlands, Sweden, Switzerland and the United Kingdom) weighted by the sum of the country's world trade during the 1972–1976 period.

3. The S&P 500 Total Return Index is based upon GFD calculations of total returns before 1971. These are estimates by GFD to calculate the values of the S&P Composite before 1971 and are not official values. GFD used data from the Cowles Commission and from S&P itself to calculate total returns for the S&P Composite using the S&P Composite Price Index and dividend yields through 1970, official monthly numbers from 1971 to 1987 and official daily data from 1988 on.

4. The trade-weighted United States dollar index is computed by the Federal Reserve. The base is 1975–1976 = 100 and 10 countries are used in computing the index. The index includes the G-10 countries (Belgium, Canada, France, Germany, Italy, Japan, Netherlands, Sweden, Switzerland and the United Kingdom) weighted by the sum of the country's world trade during the 1972–1976 period.

5. See note 3.

Chapter Fifteen: Turmoil Troubles Stocks

1. Eric S. Blake, Christopher W. Landsea and Ethan J. Gibney, "The Deadliest, Costliest and Most Intense United States Tropical Cyclones from 1851 and 2010 (And Other Frequently Requested Hurricane Facts)," NOAA Technical Memorandum NWS NHC-6, August 2011.

2. Ibid.

3. Global Financial Data, Inc., as of 6/27/2012. S&P 500 Total Return Index from 01/31/1926 to 12/31/2011. The S&P 500 Total Return Index is based upon GFD calculations of total returns before 1971. These are estimates by GFD to calculate the values of the S&P Composite before 1971 and are not official values. GFD used data from the Cowles Commission and from S&P itself to calculate total returns for the S&P Composite using the S&P Composite Price Index and dividend yields through 1970, official monthly numbers from 1971 to 1987 and official daily data from 1988 on.

Chapter Seventeen: Too Good to Be True

1. Alex Berenson, "Even Winners May Lose With Madoff," *New York Times*, December 18, 2008.

2. Global Financial Data, Inc., as of 07/10/2012; S&P 500 Total Return Index annualized returns from 12/31/1925 to 12/31/2011 is 9.7%. The S&P 500 Total Return Index is based upon GFD calculations of total returns before 1971. These are estimates by GFD to calculate the values of the S&P Composite before 1971 and are not official values. GFD used data from the Cowles Commission and from

S&P itself to calculate total returns for the S&P Composite using the S&P Composite Price Index and dividend yields through 1970, official monthly numbers from 1971 to 1987 and official daily data from 1988 on.

3. *Securities and Exchange Commission v. Stanford International Bank, et.al.*, Case No. 3:09-cv-0298-N, filed 02/29/2009.

Acknowledgments

————————— ❦ —————————

THE LITTLE BOOK SERIES is an unstoppable force, and it is with honor I add my point of view to this unique collection. Investment myth debunking is both a hobby and a professional requirement for me. My view is it's one of the easier ways investors can start putting a serious dent in their error rate fast and start seeing better investing results. Yet, too few people even *know* they should question what they (and most people) believe to be true. Hence, a Little Book on Market Myths seems an appropriate next campaign in my war on investing mythology.

As always I must thank Lara Hoffmans, who has done the yeoman's work on this and my last six books. I get the fun part of conceptualizing, styling and editing, and she gets the drudge work of making sure the book happens.

Lara has another full-time job at my firm, and backing her up while she's focused on books for me is a very talented crew of writers, including Todd Bliman (manager of the group), Elisabeth Dellinger, Naj Srinivas and Amanda Williams. She couldn't do what she does if they weren't as good as they are. Amanda once again did double duty in editing for both content and pernicious typos. Backing up *them* and lending their own copyediting expertise are the rest of the Content team, including Mary Holdener, Emily Whitney and Jake Gamble.

Once again, Jessica Wolfe and Danielle Lynch provided all the data and graphics, overseen by Matt Schrader, who heads our research analytics team. In a data-driven book about overturning market mythology with facts and fundamentals, the data must be precise. Jessica and Danielle handled it all with professionalism and grace.

Dave Eckerly, Fab Ornani and Molly Lienesch are my crack team who assist me in PR, web marketing and branding—and helping get the word out about the book.

Andrew Teufel (Vice Chairman), Jeff Silk (also a Vice Chairman), Aaron Anderson and William Glaser join me in making portfolio decisions for my firm's clients. They didn't contribute to the book, but they certainly contribute to my views of the market. Steve Triplett and Damian Ornani run the day-to-day business of my firm—which couldn't be successful without the combined efforts of those six fine gentlemen. And if my firm weren't a success, no one would be interested in what I write.

Many thanks also to my excellent team at John Wiley & Sons. I'm not always easy to deal with, but they always graciously claim that's not so. Thanks to Laura Walsh, our very patient editor, and the rest of the team: Judy Howarth, Sharon Polese, Nancy Rothschild, Jocelyn Cordova-Wagner and Tula Batanchiev. Many thanks to Jeff Herman, my excellent agent, who led me to John Wiley & Sons.

Last and most important, my wife of 42 years, Sherrilyn, whose support and patience I'm eternally grateful for.

Ken Fisher
Woodside, CA

About the Authors

KEN FISHER is best known for his prestigious "Portfolio Strategy" column in *Forbes* magazine, where his over-28-year tenure of high-profile calls makes him the fourth-longest-running columnist in *Forbes*'s 90-plus-year history. He is the founder, Chairman and CEO of Fisher Investments, an independent global money management firm managing tens of billions for individuals and institutions globally. Fisher is ranked #271 on the 2012 *Forbes* 400 list of richest Americans and #764 on the 2012 *Forbes* Global Billionaire list. In 2010, *Investment Advisor* magazine named him among the 30 most influential individuals of the last three decades. Fisher has authored numerous professional and scholarly articles, including the award-winning "Cognitive

Biases in Market Forecasting." He has also published nine previous books, including the national bestsellers, *The Only Three Questions That Count*, *The Ten Roads to Riches*, *How to Smell a Rat*, *Debunkery* and *Markets Never Forget*, all of which are published by Wiley. Fisher has been published, interviewed and/or written about in many major American, British and German finance or business periodicals. He has a weekly column in *Focus Money*, Germany's leading weekly finance and business magazine.

LARA HOFFMANS is Vice President of Content at Fisher Investments, managing editor of MarketMinder.com, a regular contributor to Forbes.com and coauthor of the bestsellers, *The Only Three Questions That Count*, *The Ten Roads to Riches*, *How to Smell a Rat*, *Debunkery* and *Markets Never Forget*. A graduate of the University of Notre Dame, she currently lives in Camas, Washington.